The Woman in Management

Career and Family Issues

Edited by
Jennie Farley

D1606272

ILR PRESS
New York State School of
Industrial and Labor Relations
Cornell University

Cover design by Richard Rosenbaum

Library of Congress Catalog Card Number: 83-2338
ISBN: 0-87546-100-X

Library of Congress Cataloging in Publication Data
Main entry under title:

The Woman in management.

  Papers and discussion from a conference sponsored by the Extension and Public Service
Division of the New York State School of Industrial and Labor Relations and held at Cornell
University in Apr. 1982.

  Bibliography: p.
  Includes index.
  1. Women executives—United States—Congresses.
  2. Women in business—United States—Congresses.
  I. Farley, Jennie.   II. New York State School of Industrial and Labor Relations. Extension and
Public Service Division.

HF5500.3.U54W62 1983   331.4'81658'00973   83-2338
ISBN 0-87546-100-X (pbk.)

Copies may be ordered directly from

ILR Press
New York State School of Industrial
  and Labor Relations
Cornell University, Box 1000
Ithaca, NY 14853

Printed in the United States of America by Braun-Brumfield, Inc.
5432

Contents

Preface   *v*

1. Women in a Changing Economy   *1*
   Juanita M. Kreps

2. Women and Men at Work: Jockeying for Position   *12*
   Betty Lehan Harragan

3. Women Managers: Moving Up in a High Tech Society   *21*
   Rosabeth Moss Kanter

4. Panel Presentations
   Being a Manager in a Multicultural World   *37*
   Pam McAllister Johnson
   Coping with Illegal Sex Discrimination   *40*
   Linda Bartlett
   The Single Woman: Moving Up by Moving Around   *45*
   Carol Kiryluk
   Dual Career Couples: How the Company Can Help   *49*
   Eleanor Byrnes
   Working Couples and Child Care   *54*
   Patricia M. Oesterle
   Does Becoming a Parent Mean Falling Off the Fast Track?   *57*
   Gail Bryant Osterman
   One Family's Decision: A Leave of Absence   *61*
   Margaret Coffey
   Personal Choices   *65*
   Deborah K. Smith
   Discussion   *69*

5. Recommended Readings   *73*
   Jennie Farley

Index   *97*

"Women's future careers will be far better than any of us dared hope as recently as a decade ago."

—JUANITA M. KREPS

"Women have not been successful up to now because most of us have been playing solitaire in the middle of a football field."

—BETTY LEHAN HARRAGAN

"The problem is not that we don't know how to play on teams. It is that it is very hard to play on a team that doesn't want you on it."

—ROSABETH MOSS KANTER

Preface

Problems women encounter and present as managers were discussed at a conference at Cornell University in April 1982. Representatives of forty-four public and private employers in New York and neighboring states met with faculty and graduate students in labor relations, business, economics, and related disciplines. One aim was to bring together those who deal with these issues on a day-to-day basis with those who study them.

This conference was sponsored by the Extension and Public Service Division of the New York State School of Industrial and Labor Relations with partial support from four corporations: Xerox of Rochester; Aetna Life and Casualty Foundation of Hartford, Connecticut; IBM Corporation of Armonk, New York; and Mobil Oil Corporation of New York City. A fifth supporter was a committee known as CWEP: the New York State Governor's Office of Employee Relations and the Civil Service Association Joint Labor/Management Committee on the Work Environment and Productivity.

First impetus for the conference came, however, from women students who were wrestling with decisions about their future commitments to careers and to family life. As graduate student Kathleen Weslock noted in her remarks at the conference reception, "There are women who don't like to think about women's issues. They think of themselves as professionals, not women professionals. We can all understand that. But some of us feel that all the questions are not answered yet. How do women actually manage full-time careers and still have time for family life? Are women really being promoted into top management posts? Are employers interested enough in hiring women to change some of the employment practices that have been a problem for women in the past?"

Graduate students in many disciplines proved to have similar concerns; they joined forces to support the conference.[1] Women's organizations in the community proved to share deep concerns about women in management: how could they join with the students to discuss their insights and share their experiences? As Dean Charles Rehmus of the School of Industrial and Labor Relations noted in his welcome, the program represented welcome cooperation between town and gown.[2]

Three major speakers—an economist, a sociologist, and a management consultant—each brought a different perspective to the question of women's prospects as managers. Each also had concrete, practical suggestions for the women attending the sessions, some of which will be found in the discussion summaries at the end of the chapters.

In chapter 1 of this volume, economist Juanita Kreps, former

---

1. Cooperating organizations included the Industrial and Labor Relations Women's Caucus, Cornell student chapter of the American Home Economics Association, Cornell Society of Women Engineers, Cornell Women in Communications, Women's Association of the Graduate School of Business and Public Administration, Cornell's Women's Studies Program, Women's Law Coalition, and Cornell Women's Caucus.

2. Supporting organizations, other than student groups, were the Ithaca branch of the American Association of University Women (AAUW), Business and Professional Women's Club of Ithaca, Cornell Women's Club of Tompkins County, Ithaca Zonta, Professional Skills Roster, and the Tompkins County National Organization for Women (NOW). Other supporters included the student honorary societies of Mortarboard and Quill & Dagger, the University Lecture Committee at Cornell, the Provost's Advisory Committee on the Status of Women at Cornell, and, from farther afield, the Syracuse University chapter of the Society for the Advancement of Management and the interest group on women of the national Academy of Management.

secretary of commerce,[3] traces the effects of demographic and social changes on the role of women in the economy. Women are in paying jobs to stay, she states, predicting that the drive for comparable pay will continue until the gap between women's earnings and men's is substantially reduced. Why has progress been slow? Not, she emphasizes, because of individual shortcomings of women but because of the other factors she reviews. Women and men joining the work force in the near future have the disadvantage of entering an uncertain economy but they also have advantages, Kreps says. For one thing, there are fewer entrants, thus less competition than was the case in the past. For another, job discrimination has been greatly reduced. There are still problems, she acknowledges, but she urges women to look forward to the challenges of the battles ahead with excitement, not apprehension. Otherwise, the game is not worth the candle.

Chapter 2 presents management consultant Betty Lehan Harragan's thesis that women must learn the rules of the business world and learn how to play on a team. Harragan administers a short quiz which may convince some readers (as it did some listeners) that women and men bring such different experiences to the work place that women are critically disadvantaged in a man's environment. Harragan hammers home the fact that women and men do different work and that many women do not even know the difference. She emphasizes that political action is vital if the status of all women in American society is to be improved.

In chapter 3, sociologist Rosabeth Moss Kanter analyzes the world of work in terms of the advent of high technology. In the high tech world, Kanter says, work assignments are ambiguous, managers are interdependent as never before, and there is local

---

3. In 1982 Kreps was only the sixth woman to have served in the U.S. Cabinet. The others were Patricia Roberts Harris, Secretary of Health, Education and Welfare; Carla Anderson Hills, Secretary of Housing and Urban Development; Oveta Culp Hobby, Secretary of Health, Education and Welfare; Shirley Mount Hufstedler, Secretary of the Department of Education; and Frances Perkins, Secretary of Labor, later a member of the faculty of the New York State School of Industrial and Labor Relations, Cornell University.

autonomy which did not exist in old-style corporate-headquarters-centered organizations. To be effective, managers and other leaders must understand power, Kanter holds. She defines "job power" as accessible to those in positions where they can exercise discretion, where they are visible, and where the task is immediately relevant to the organization's critical priorities. Managers can gain what she calls "relationship power" from sponsors, from coworkers, and from subordinates. The extent to which women will be powerful in the future will depend on the extent to which they are able to make their way into positions with these attributes, and not be isolated or neglected there.

In chapter 4, the panelists' talks are presented, together with the discussion they elicited. Publisher Pam McAllister Johnson tells how she dealt with coworkers who felt that she was disadvantaged by being black and female; attorney Linda Bartlett focuses on the law as a tool for women in a world where fierce discrimination still exists; personnel executive Carol Kiryluk reflects on the advantages and disadvantages of being free from family ties as one makes one's way up the corporate ladder. Banker Eleanor Byrnes describes ways in which corporations like hers are seeking to accommodate to mobility problems that come about when two professionals are serious both about their careers and about their commitment to one another. Patricia Oesterle, an attorney in private practice, lays out the challenges of remaining professionally active when one has small children. Marketing expert Gail Bryant Osterman describes a solution she and her husband have found; she is candid about what it has cost them in terms not only of money but of peace as a family. Margaret Coffey tells how she came to decide to take a leave of absence while her children are babies—a decision that took a certain courage to make and to defend before a group of young women who could not believe such a thing would be necessary in the 1980s. Personnel manager Deborah K. Smith describes some of the trade-offs she makes in her busy life. Those present asked the panelists hard questions, which were answered thoughtfully and carefully.

Chapter 5 presents a brief review of the research about and advice books for women managers. An annotated bibliography of writings that appear to be the most sensible and useful is included.

To talk about these issues openly rather than pretending that women professionals and managers are not women is surely a step in the right direction. Each presentation elicited spirited discussion— from the extent to which minority women are keeping up with their white sisters to the efficacy of discussion groups for women contemplating pregnancy to the effect the Moral Majority will have on women's prospects as managers. Only one commentator seemed out of step with the others. Her statement—that, on the one hand, women would be corrupted if they sold out to the corporate world and that, on the other, the only way for women to get power is to seize it, using violence if necessary—was heard out politely but disregarded.

The concerns that prompted this conference were practical and down-to-earth. The solutions presented were framed not as commands or precepts that all must follow but ideas that might work for some. The senior women were unanimous in emphasizing that all is not glamour and ease and equality for women in the early 1980s. It is not. There are still barriers to be demolished and they will not go down easily. But go down they will.

JENNIE FARLEY

CHAPTER 1

Women in a Changing Economy

Juanita M. Kreps

In the early 1980s, an undergraduate interviewed by the *New York Times* was quite certain about one aspect of her role. The *Times* reporter pointed out that "she could be the symbol of everything the women's movement fought to win. A senior at Princeton, she has just won a Rotary fellowship to study in France. She expects to attend business school and work in international finance. But when Mary Anne Citrino marries and has her children, she plans to quit whatever job she has for eight years to become a full-time mother... 'If I can't give my children one hundred percent,' Miss Citrino said, 'I'd rather not be a mother at all.'" The article goes on to report that of 3,000 college students interviewed, 77 percent of the women and 84 percent of the men said mothers should not work at

Juanita M. Kreps served as U.S. Secretary of Commerce from January 1977 to December 1979. An emeritus professor of Duke University, Kreps is a graduate of Berea College and holds the Ph.D. in economics from Duke. A member of Phi Beta Kappa, she has been the recipient of many honorary degrees. She was named James B. Duke Professor of Economics at Duke in 1972 and appointed vice president there in 1973, a post she held until 1977. Author of *Women and the American Economy* (1976) and *Sex in the Marketplace: American Women at Work* (1971), Kreps has also written textbooks on economics. She was awarded the 1981 Achievement Award by the American Association of University Women.

all, or work only part time, until their children are five years old.[1] These young people seem not to be aware that their attitude is at odds with the trends of the past three decades.

Not surprisingly, the article provoked a spirited rebuttal. An editorial chided the young women interviewed for assuming that the fruits of the feminist struggle for access to universities like Princeton, careers in law or finance, and equal treatment in the work force called for no commitment on their part. A letter writer wondered what employer would "compensate at rates equal to men a woman who thinks she deserves eight years of maternity leave." Others wondered what young men could earn enough to support the life style envisaged by these women, or how a highly trained and motivated career woman could expect to step out of a career and into the home, and then back again, with no guilt, loss of identity, or slipping on the career ladder.

A further rebuttal came in the form of a new study, this time at Radcliffe, which suggested that young women and men viewed their career and family prospects somewhat differently. In this case, career plans were found to be much the same for women and men students, practically all of them saying they would go beyond the bachelor's degree to study for master's, doctoral, medical, law, or business degrees. About the same percentage of women as men planned to follow the careers of their fathers and a similar, though smaller, proportion opted to follow their mothers' professions. Although practically all wanted to marry, more men than women said they wanted children. Most women, and one-fourth of the men, preferred part-time work when children were infants and preschoolers.

I cite these studies to emphasize the ambivalence in attitudes toward women's careers. It is also important to remind ourselves of the reasons for the changes in women's lives and their aspirations. For, despite the obvious changes, one often hears the plaintive query: What is happening to women? What is happening to women today reflects major shifts in society—changes in family size and life style, in the division of labor in the home and in the work place, in our expectations for men and women. We are no longer members of

---

1. Dina Kleiman, "Many Young Women Now Say They'd Pick Family over Career," *New York Times*, December 28, 1980, p. 1.

that blue-collar, male-headed family of four living in the suburban house of the nineteen forties and fifties, any more than we belong to the large, three-generational farm family of the early twentieth century. Yet nostalgia for those earlier family styles pervades much of our thinking. Industrial development, which brought us from the large farm to the small computer, has been paralleled by changing patterns of births and deaths and, more recently, by the emergence of a communication network that constantly dramatizes an ever higher standard of living. These shifts have profoundly altered our domestic lives and our working patterns. In the wake of such sweeping moves, it should not surprise us at all that the lives of women, along with those of men, would be revolutionized.

Under the impact of this quiet revolution, the traditional taboos—"Yes, she's an excellent accountant, but what happens when she becomes pregnant?" or "How can I promote her if she can't move to another city?" or "My clients simply won't accept a woman engineer"—are fading from use. And the stereotype of the mentally deficient female is not as freely bandied about as it was a decade ago when a male student challenged my credentials as a director of the New York Stock Exchange because, he said, his mother didn't know anything about money. When I confessed to him that in fact I did find the securities markets complex but that it had never occurred to me that intellectual capacity was sex related, he grumbled, "I don't know about all that. But I know my mother."

Management expert Peter Drucker underscored the gap between perception and reality when he posed this question: "How much longer will TV comedies feature the little woman who cannot balance her checkbook when more than half of all students in accounting courses are female?"[2]

But let us not dwell on the limited access we suffered in the past. All of us are happy to leave that chapter of history to turn instead to what is sure to be a bright future for career women in the professions and in the corporate world. This view was represented in a recent *Wall Street Journal* cartoon, which, in a twist on a traditional theme, showed a woman with her arm around a young girl, looking out a

---

2. Peter M. Drucker, "Working Women: Unmaking the Nineteenth Century," *Wall Street Journal*, July 6, 1981, p. 12.

window and pointing to an expanse of factory buildings. "Some day, dear, all this will be yours."

Women's future careers will be far better than any of us dared hope as recently as a decade ago. The reasons for the vastly improved picture are partly demographic and economic. To some significant degree, too, the bright outlook results from judicial and legislative actions that grew out of the civil rights and women's movements.

The demographic changes have produced more childless marriages, more one-adult and small families. The number of women heads of households has increased sharply. Women's life expectancy continues to exceed that of men, and women are living alone for much longer periods, both in youth and in later years. As a result of these patterns, many economic and legal questions have to be addressed. Issues such as property rights; custody and child support; tax policy as it relates to child care, alimony, and dependency, as well as to marital status; and retirement provisions under public and private pensions are being reexamined.

Consider some future effects of these demographic developments. Employers who had large pools of workers to draw from during the sixties and seventies will face different labor market conditions in the eighties and nineties. As the numbers of new entrants to the work force shrink, it will be necessary for employers to make new efforts to keep women at work, to train them as managers or skilled workers in nontraditional areas. Changes will have to be made in personnel policies that were designed for men whose families move freely with them and who did not require child care or maternity leave.

These issues have already surfaced. Indeed, two of the biggest fringe benefit issues of the seventies—maternity and child care provisions and equal monthly retirement benefits for women—emerged because personnel practice was inadequate to deal with the needs of working women. Other problems—career timing, work scheduling—must also be handled at the corporate level if business is to retain highly trained women.

In addition to benefit questions, employers are now confronted with new questions of worker mobility. A working wife is less free to move in accordance with her husband's job needs; moreover, she often needs to move to further her own career. Employers have so far taken slight account of a spouse's relocation problem, and only recently have firms begun to offer married women promotion when changes in location are required. The prevailing assumption has been that women with families would not move. Yet a woman's advance to a top corporate job often necessitates her moving, which may conflict with her husband's career goals.

In short, demographic changes that bring fewer young people into the work force will trigger new corporate policies. The packages of "goodies" offered to young men to keep them from being hired away are not altogether persuasive to women. Instead of worrying about meeting equal opportunity laws, employers will need to develop policies that improve the contributions and the morale of women employees.

While all these good things are happening, what are women doing to advance their careers? First of all, they are preparing themselves to take advantage of a new and different world. It is not news that law and business schools are now enrolling almost as many women as men and medical schools' enrollees are one-fourth to one-third female. With these models before them, women will stretch their aspirations and their numbers in these professions will grow. Changes in undergraduate education are occurring as well, calling for new staffing and new attitudes among faculties.

Easy assumptions that most women students will study the humanities and then go into teaching and social work have already been discarded. Many educational institutions have not fully adjusted to the resulting implications for faculty composition. They keep asking: Is the shift of interest toward law and business a permanent one? Or does it reflect a temporary concern on the part of women and men over the shortage of jobs?

The answers should be abundantly clear. We now know that most women are in paying jobs to stay; that women's work lives are approaching men's; that the drive for comparable pay will continue until the earnings gap is substantially reduced; and that, in contrast to the World War II era and the postwar era, when women returned to hearth and home as quickly as possible, most young women today take for granted that they will have both jobs and marriages.

What, then, are the constraints? If it is all this simple and easy, why are so many women having a hard time? Which are the real problems and which are the frivolous concerns? The problems lie not in women's individual shortcomings, but in the global changes that are taking place, including economic ones. Although these problems are not intractable, there is a great deal of hand-wringing. Everywhere, gloom and doom prevail. Instead of solutions, we hear criticism; rather than developing practical programs, we make lists of what went wrong and who is to blame. Economist Alice Rivlin, director of the Congressional Budget, has noted that

As a nation, we are luxuriating in a massive national gripe session in which everyone is enjoying telling everyone else that nothing works and that no one is competent, especially those whose misfortune it is to lead the national government. There is general agreement that we need stronger political leaders, smarter advisors, a better class of international enemies, and more predictable volcanoes.[3]

We continue to look to economic policymakers to deal with today's recession, unemployment, high interest rates, and persistent inflation, even if our confidence in their judgment wanes in troubled times. How optimistic should we be that present public policies, along with the decisions being made in the private sector, will turn the economy around as promised? What should we expect in the longer term? Beyond the recession and all the human problems in its wake, most of us look for reasonably good growth in the 1980s. To achieve this growth, we need a more coherent set of economic policies. There is a fundamental conflict between a restrictive monetary policy designed to reduce inflation by holding interest rates high and a fiscal policy that promises a balanced budget, while cutting taxes and increasing spending on defense.

Some of our longer run problems will persist into the 1980s, long after the current recession has run its course. There is widespread agreement that economic growth immediately following the recession will be sluggish, both here and throughout Europe. International competition for markets will grow and trade wars are a threat under conditions of slow growth and unemployment. Amer-

---

3. Carol Rigolot, *A Vision of America* (Washington, D.C.: American Council of Life Insurance, Education and Community Services, 1981), p. 1.

ican industry has suffered productivity losses when compared with the records of our foreign competitors and in comparison with our own past records. Heavy expenditures for defense and growing expenditures for entitlement programs will strain federal budgets. It is in this economic setting that women beginning their careers will have to find their way. Although college-educated women are unlikely to face the threat of permanent unemployment, they are not assured of quick access to the jobs of their choice. But they do have two important advantages over the women and men who graduated before them. One, there are fewer people joining the work force now, which will make jobs easier to find; and two, the job discrimination so rampant in the sixties and seventies has been greatly reduced.

In this good-news–bad-news scenario, I find the future far more promising for women than ever before, despite the probable state of the economy in the near term. Demography is on their side. Legislation and public opinion are supportive. It is a freer, more equitable society. Best of all, it is rapidly becoming a society in which women as well as men share the privilege and the responsibility for finding solutions to the problems we all face.

There will continue to be barriers, of course, the immediate one being the soft labor market generated by a slowed-down economy. Nothing would do more to enhance the opportunities for women and men than a return to prosperity and economic growth. In the meantime, the challenge is to maintain our momentum in a period when the economy is slack and when the rules of the marketplace are often confusing to women who are so often performing new roles. Ambivalence is everywhere, most especially in our own minds. For example, we often lack the confidence in ourselves and the system; we have to learn to trust ourselves more. We are not yet ready to risk failure, but surely we are allowed to fail—as men do. That is part of the secret of their success. Some (though surely not all) of us are uncomfortable with authority, since we have so seldom held positions that carried the mantle of power. We do not yet know how we will handle it. Since we are so often long on compassion, however, I suspect we will manage power with grace.

While you are learning to operate successfully and make contributions on the job, the job itself is constantly changing. You are likely to follow not one but several different career paths; some of your most exciting prospects may be outside the field in which you begin your career. I would urge you to be willing to make those leaps, even if they are into frighteningly different areas. You don't have to carry it to extreme, as I did — from academia to business affiliations to government, then back to the corporate and foundation world. But try to avoid the easy assumption that you can operate in only one field.

Finally, a word on morale along the way. I hope we will bring to our careers a sense of excitement and anticipation, rather than apprehension. Let's play a bit more, for surely it is a glorious time to be a woman. We can now do things that our mothers, even our older sisters, were never allowed. Our freedom to choose, though restrained by the realities of the job market, is far greater than some of us ever thought possible. We should not lose sight of these gains, nor fail to delight in them, as we proceed to demolish the remaining barriers.

It will not do us any good to win this battle for equality if we forget to enjoy the fruits of our victory.

Discussion

Will the philosophy of the new right affect women's opportunities for advancement in management? Dr. Kreps acknowledged that this could be a problem, in part because many in that camp have a more traditional view of women's role than many young women find convenient and in part because they sometimes accuse women jobseekers of generating unemployment. There is a tradition, Kreps observed, of pitting unemployed groups against one another. In the 1930s and indeed until after World War II, women school teachers who were married were told to leave their jobs because it was said that they were displacing male breadwinners. Now, even if this were true, given the number of women heads of households today and the need for women in many families to work, the argument would make no sense, Kreps said. But this is not true: women do not displace men. That is not the way our economy works, she explained. When the economy is booming, there are not enough people to fill the jobs. When it is slack, unemployment is rampant. Will the Moral Majority retard women's progress at work? Kreps felt it would not because while the new right has influence, it does not have the power. "I believe," Kreps said, "that we should save our fire for more important battles than trying to fight the Moral Majority. The important battles are getting decent jobs, bringing about real equity in the work place, and showing how good and fair we can be when we get there."

It used to be the case, Kreps noted, that when a woman got a good job it was thought that she must have gotten it, not on merit, but because of reverse discrimination, because she was favored. That myth is dying out, though not as fast as some of us might like. Kreps remarked that when she left public life, one of her colleagues asked what she was planning to do. She said she planned to go back and serve on corporate boards, just as she had before. Her colleague said, "Y'all will just be a token." Kreps allowed as how a person with a Ph.D. in economics and decades of experience could scarcely be taken for a token.

The Equal Rights Amendment is an important symbol, Kreps said, in answer to another question. As a society, we ought to be ashamed that it was not passed long ago. It is just as important to homemakers as it is to women who work for pay, she remarked.

In answer to a question about equal pay for work of comparable value, Kreps said that this is an important issue and one that will not go away. Nor will it be easily resolved, she said. Since Biblical times, when women were said to be worth thirty shekels versus men's worth of fifty shekels, there has been a pay gap. In 1982, she said, women as a group earn about 60 percent of what men as a group do.

Another listener brought the speaker back to her original example of the undergraduates who were wrestling with the problem of planning both careers and families. The problem is a difficult one, Kreps acknowledged. She noted that, so long as women have the major responsibility for child care, women may take longer to reach their full potential at work than men do. But, she noted, women do live longer. In the meantime, both women and men should be open to job changes. Narrow specialists will be at a disadvantage in the competition, she said.

How would the speaker improve the state of the economy if she could? It is essential to get the deficits down, to cut expenditures, to reduce defense spending, and not to try to make changes in income tax, she said. Raising excise taxes would help, she added. There must be less spending on defense and more tax revenues.

One questioner wondered if, so long as there are men available, corporations would ever make concessions to women? In one sense, Kreps said, we have now won equal treatment. Employers treat women the same as they do men. This is a great improvement over the past, when women were disadvantaged in the competition just because they were women. But now we have another battle to fight: we have to get employers to treat us differently because we are women. We have every right to demand child care, the advantages of part-time work, flextime, and so forth. She noted that these concessions are not being made very rapidly in universities, which, she suggested delicately, may move at a slower pace than employers elsewhere.

The state of the economy is a constraint on careers of both women and men, she acknowledged. In answer to a question about sexual harassment at work, Kreps said that, in her generation, women accepted as part of the battle certain behaviors on the part of men. "If I hear of such things now," she said, "I take the place apart." Senior women have a responsibility to help younger women fight sexual harassment. The young are vulnerable to job loss if they complain so they must depend on senior women, who are secure, to help them.

As a final piece of counsel, Kreps advised all women and men to only take on issues they thought they could win. There is much to be done, she said; we have to pick our fights carefully.

CHAPTER 2

Women and Men at Work: Jockeying for Position

Betty Lehan Harragan

I am happy to be here today at a conference where women speak to other women on how to get ahead on the job. This is still a new phenomenon. In fact, the very idea that women should be interested in helping themselves rather than helping everybody in the world except themselves is still a revolutionary concept and one that is viewed as slightly subversive in many circles, even now. Another reason I am happy to be here is that I consider myself to be one of you. I have spent my entire life as a career professional woman.

It used to be thought that the reason women have never gotten ahead at work is the shortness of their tenure in the work force. But I have known thousands of women who have worked every bit as long as men; they had long tenure but no success.

Betty Lehan Harragan is the principal in Betty Harragan & Affiliates, a consulting firm devoted to equal employment and promotion of women. Author of *Games Mother Never Taught You: Corporate Gamesmanship for Women* (New York: Rawson Associates, 1977), Harragan writes a monthly column on the problems of working women which appeared in *Saavy* magazine until November 1982 and in *Working Woman* magazine since then. A television film based on Harragan's book was aired on CBS Television in December 1982. A sought-after lecturer at conferences and conventions, Harragan earned the B.A. from Marquette University and the M.A. from Columbia University.

Reviewing my own career, it sometimes seems as though I spent most of my time being turned down for all the jobs I really wanted. Sometimes I think I hit my head on just about every discriminatory ceiling around. I used to have a two-inch-thick file of letters from major corporations around the country that said things like, "Thank you for sending your resume; your qualifications are wonderful; thank you for your interest in our company; I am sure you will find a place where your talents will be appreciated but we are sorry, we don't hire women." It is difficult, perhaps, for young women today to believe that that is the way it was. Eight to ten years ago, there were no women except clerical workers in any of the big industrial companies. There were no women on television; none in the stock exchange, the big financial institutions, or the banks; no women in account management in advertising agencies; no women partners in accounting firms or legal firms; no women in sales anywhere; and certainly no women in senior academic posts in colleges and universities.

In 1972 when I started my own business as a consultant specializing in upward mobility for women, I thought the situation had changed. After all, that was the year when the Equal Rights Amendment finally made it out of the committee in the U.S. Congress and was sent to the states for ratification. That was the year the Supreme Court decided it was not unconstitutional for the Congress to have passed a law that said women should be paid the same as men doing identical work in the same office, company, or plant. I thought that the antidiscrimination laws—Title VII of the Civil Rights Act, Title IX of the Education Amendments Act—were mandates to be obeyed. But I found out soon enough that the equal employment laws were merely new and difficult challenges for the gamesmen of business who sought to evade rather than obey them.

Actually, little has changed today. Discrimination against women used to be blatant, outright, and expressed. Today, it is subtle, covert, and universally denied. One way discrimination against women is expressed in 1982 is the word "qualified." Employers say, "There just are no qualified women" or "No qualified women ever apply" or "There are no women qualified for this level of management." Not only employers but executive recruiters say that. One result is that colleges, business groups, and many commercial organizations are all leaping into the breach, saying they will train women to overcome this genetic handicap. Women are being taught to "develop their managerial style" and to become more assertive— never aggressive, which is not "lady-like." This kind of abacadabra does not jibe with my twenty-five years of experience in business: I never once saw any male colleague of mine rush around to first improve his personality or his management style before he got promoted to be my boss.

Despite the allegation that women lack qualifications, all around the country I see women who are well educated, exceedingly competent, dedicated to their employers or their professions, really working hard, confident of their own skills and abilities, and, of course, increasingly ambitious. Yet, in spite of all these personal and professional qualifications, they are still not being considered on a par with men. Do you call that sex discrimination? That particular disease is alive and thriving in our society. In fact, in the 1980s, it is reaching epidemic proportions as many of the gains women have made in the last decade are threatened with extinction.

The other side of the coin is that there is a certain knowledge men have that women seem not to have: information about the business world. The business world as it exists now and as it is being redesigned for the new economic situation of the 1980s was developed by men, for men, so they understand it. Even modestly successful men seem to know intuitively that the business of working is a lifelong game and that success means winning as many points as possible in that game. Women, on the other hand, seldom realize that they are playing a game, much less what kind of game, and never mind what the rules are. There is a good reason why women do not know: the rules are, by and large, unwritten.

One of my aims in writing *Games Mother Never Taught You* was to identify some of these operating rules so that women would have a sporting chance to get in there and play. The game is real. It has a theory, a clearly defined game board or playing field, stringent rules and regulations, prescribed moves to get ahead, severe penalties for fouls or infractions of the rules, a code of conduct, and, above all, it has a public scoreboard where the points are racked up in dollars and promotions for all the world to see. Success is indeed determined by how well one plays the games, not at all by how well one does any particular job. To understand how adult women can be so naive about office politics (as the game is popularly called), you have to appreciate that boys and girls in our society are brought up, even to this day, in two entirely different cultures. When little girls grow up and take a job, it is as if they are instantly transported to some exotic South Seas island where they don't know the terrain, they have no friends, they are not familiar with the customs, nobody has given them an accurate map, they can't read the signposts, and they do not understand the language, even though a lot of the words sound familiar.

In one respect, then, management men are right: most women are unqualified in the sense that they know nothing about how business or government or academia operate at the top administrative or managerial levels. As women, we have been totally excluded from that kind of experience. Instead of recognizing what the source of our problems actually is, we tend to look for weaknesses within ourselves. We are advised to deal with our anxieties and guilt and to examine our motivations for working. When did you last hear any man asked to explain his motivations for working? When are men asked what they really want to do in this world? When are they instructed to make endless lists of goals?

Young women tell me that a popular interview question is, "Tell me, where do you want to be five years from now?" Often women are urged to go back to school and get more degrees. This is curious counsel when you consider that in 1982 women college graduates earn less money than white male high school dropouts. In short, women are taught to look at their careers through microscopes trained on themselves, while their ambitious high performance male colleagues are looking at the job through high-powered binoculars, trained on that playing field.

Here is a test I like to give women to predict their Business Games Quotient. How many have ever served in any branch of the military? (The answer is usually about two yeses to ninety-eight no's.) How many ever played basketball, baseball, football, or volleyball? (Usually a good majority.) How many played those sports on a coached team in some kind of structured league? (A minority, but more say yes now than used to be the case.) How many played "girls' rules"? (Almost all the sportswomen.) How many have gotten a promotion during the last two years? (Increasingly larger numbers.) How many asked for a specific dollar amount raise in the last twelve months? (Generally 10 to 20 percent.) Of those who asked, how many got what they asked for? (Most.) Raise-seekers are starting to play the game, but if they knew the rules just a bit better, they would realize that they are not asking for half enough. How many are in line jobs? (Typically 95 percent don't know what that means.) That's a loaded question because anyone who is not absolutely positive whether she has a line job or a staff job is instantly at a terrible disadvantage compared to male colleagues who seem to know this before they know anything else. Line jobs are where the action is, where the money is, where the power is. A rule of thumb to identify line jobs: those are the jobs for which women are deemed to be "unqualified."

In order to figure out where the line jobs are in your organization, you must understand the layout of the game board, or to be more precise, the playing field. The layout is modeled very precisely after the military hierarchy. The minute you work for a salary in any kind of organization, you are in the army, know it or not, like it or not. Being in the army means you are subject to all the strict rules of protocol: deference to authority, respect for rank and status, obedience to orders, and conformance to the chain-of-command dictates. To whom do you report? It is as simple as that. In a hierarchy, everyone reports to one person and one person only. The military hierarchy is shaped like a triangle or pyramid: at the top is either the five-star general or the chief executive officer. Down at the broad bottom base are the buck privates. Most of us are located in the lower middle ranges, one of the many tiers. The most important fact to know is that all power in a hierarchy flows from the top down; like water, it never flows uphill.

The line jobs in the army are the combat troops, the fighting arm. Everybody else is in a staff job; all the technical and specialty branches, supply recruitment, procurement of materiel, and so forth are support services. Their function is to support the fighting troops whose objective is to win the war.

In private industry, the objective is to make money. In government, academia, and the nonprofit sector, the aim is still money but in these cases not by selling something for profit but by accumulating money from other sources: appropriations, grants, donations, budget allocations, whatever. In all civilian organizations, the combat troops can be said to be those in money-making operations. Big organizations can have several profit centers. In private industry, the "combat troops" are either in sales-marketing or production, or, increasingly, in high-level finance departments that make money on money. Everybody else is staff. In a recession, staff departments are where the first cuts are made. Typical staff departments are: accounting, personnel (or, if you prefer the fancy name, human resources), public relations (often renamed corporate communications), advertising, research, consumer affairs, customer relations, data processing, office administration, planning, and legal departments. These are the very departments where women are, in great numbers. Many of the success stories of women's progress in the business world are in those departments —where women have always been—in the staff jobs, away from the line jobs where the action is.

A crucial distinction is that staff jobs never have policy decision-making authority. Even the departmental vice president, which is as high as one can go in a staff function, can merely advise, persuade, suggest, or recommend programs to a line officer who always retains final authority. Therefore, I believe we must encourage younger women to aim for the line jobs and divert them from staff functions, which are rapidly turning in female ghettos.

The actual games that go on in both staff and line jobs are modeled after competitive team sports. Did you ever wonder where boys get that early childhood training for business so that, when they get out into the work world, they have an almost subliminal feel for what is going on? They get it on the playground, in the gym, from the coaches, on the varsity team. If you don't believe that, listen closely when businessmen or politicians talk. You will hear military and sports jargon everywhere.

Let us take one example: the word *team*. Many of you may be hearing the phrase in your own job: "We're all on the same team," "This department is like a professional team," "We have to improve our teamwork on this project." Now, if you ask a group of women what a team is, they will usually say it means: "Everybody should cooperate to get the job done," "Everybody pitches in, doing whatever they can to help others," "Everybody supports everybody else," "Everyone is responsible for the team result, thus, you have to cover for somebody who slacks off." But if you ask a ten-year-old boy what a team is, he will often respond in baseball terminology. "There's a pitcher, a catcher, a first baseman, second baseman, third baseman, fielders, and so on." Notice, there is nothing vague about that description, no generalized vagaries about "a bunch of guys supporting one another." By the time they are ten, little boys know— and they don't even know they know, but they do—that a team is a very rigid structure and has a prescribed function, that each player covers his own position and nobody else's.

It is instructive to watch a baseball team on a playing field. You will notice that a lot of guys stand around doing nothing most of the time. But you will also notice that the first baseman does not, in the midst of a game, run over to the mound to pitch for the pitcher. Nor does a second baseman offer to assist an overworked third baseman by covering both bases for the rest of the inning. Hardly.

Let's take another example: the word *coach*. The coach assigns the positions, gives the orders, runs the team, makes the decisions, coordinates the action. Would a coach ever run out and take over for a shortstop? Of course not. The coach is the manager, not a player.

Once you begin to understand the gamesmanship concept, you will see that your most important relationship at work is to your immediate boss. That person is not only your connecting link in the chain of command, but your top sergeant or your team coach. So you cannot ever publicly demean, insult, or refuse to obey that person because rank must be respected. Even if the *person* in that rank is your idea of a jerk, you must respect the job rank. Thus, it is always important to pick your immediate boss very, very carefully.

Then, or course, comes the matter of your salary. In a game where the score is kept in dollars and cents, nobody is going to run around dispensing little gifts of points. In order to get paid what you are worth, you have to ask. You can never let a day go by without thinking about money: your own money, your department's money, the unit's budget, the organization's money, your boss's money, and your coworkers' salaries. This is, in my opinion, the only legitimate subject for a female grapevine: constant, cold-blooded discussion and analysis of what jobs are worth in a competitive male market and how much your services are worth in comparison. I am convinced that women can learn to be as good players as men because games of power depend on brains, not brawn. And the brains women have in plenty. Women have not been successful up to now because most of us have been playing solitaire in the middle of a football field wondering why we are being trampled to death. We have not been reared to know that if you want to compete in a team sport, the first thing you have to have is a team. Of course, you don't learn a new and unfamiliar game overnight. Skill develops as you play this game every day at work. Most women have much more gaming background than they give themselves credit for. The problem is that they have not been playing to win.

In that connection, I want to leave you with a warning: none of us, despite the greatest personal accomplishments, will ever get equal pay and equal consideration in the work place until women are recognized as constitutional citizens of our own country, until we are persons, not objects, under the law. The Equal Rights Amendment must be our first priority. If you think the ERA is a lost cause, you have not caught on to the concept of gamesmanship. Did you ever see a football game where the players looked at the clock and said, "Oh, well, we are so far behind, we can't win, so let's just all head for the showers?" No, the first thing men learn is that the game is not over until the last bell rings. Too, no matter what the score, there is always another game coming up. ERA II will give us all the chance to get in there and play!

There is another important element in any career, which I can only wish you: good luck.

Discussion

In answer to a question about the crucial difference between a staff job and a line job, Ms. Harragan gave the example of sales work. That, she said, is the very epitome of a line position and one that women should be striving for. In fact, she said, "You can say that nobody ever got to the top of anything without sales experience."

One problem with our upbringing, Harragan said, is that we have not quite realized that the paid job market is impersonal. We have thought somehow that if we were good and polite, our worth would be recognized. Not so. She urged women to build female teams and to put on forceful pressure to have more women coworkers. Would women as a group have a good effect on corporations and the way they do business? Harragan was inclined to think such hopes were unrealistic. In fact, she remarked, the only way women at the top can change anything is if they are empowered from below. If junior women support the women managers, the prospect for change is better.

Citing the struggle for the Equal Rights Amendment, she said she felt very strongly that it is an example of gigantic game play. Women do not know the rules yet, she said. We must play hard; we must learn who made things happen in each of the states where ERA I was not ratified and we must make things happen there. One significant change in the 1980s—perhaps the most important one—is that women's votes are beginning to show different patterns than men's, and they ought to, she said. "In one sense, the entire system in our country is built on the backs of women. We ought not to forget that."

CHAPTER 3

Women Managers: Moving Up in a High Tech Society

Rosabeth Moss Kanter

The job world today is already different from our classic expectations; I believe it is going to be increasingly different in the future. Understanding power and influence is going to be even more critical to career success in the company of the future than it is in the company of today. We have an image—and it is in most of the received wisdom about management of organizations and management theory—of organizations as rather tidy and orderly, of people being promoted through a lockstep career sequence, of knowing what one's job is, and of setting out to do that job within acceptable boundaries. It is, in short, the image of the old-style mechanistic bureaucratic organization; that is the image of the organization most of us have thought of working in.

Rosabeth Moss Kanter, professor of organization and management and of sociology at Yale University, has served as acting chair of the Sociology Department there since Fall 1982. She is also chairman of the board of Goodmeasure, Inc., a consulting firm in Cambridge, Massachusetts. Kanter earned the B.A. from Bryn Mawr College in 1964 and the Ph.D. in sociology and social psychology from the University of Michigan in 1967. Her book, *Men and Women of the Corporation* (New York: Basic, 1977) won the C. Wright Mills Award for the best book on social issues that year. Her work has appeared in many professional journals. Kanter has been a visiting professor at Brandeis, Harvard, Harvard Law School, and the Massachusetts Institute of Technology.

The high technology society has brought into being a different reality, a way of handling jobs that is sometimes confusing, even terrifying. But it also provides a great deal of potential for those people who are independent and autonomous and who understand how to acquire and exercise power. Let me first sketch out some of the characteristics of high tech firms whether they are in silicon valley, in Minneapolis, in Fairfield County, or in New York. Then I will review how power is acquired and exercised in organizations and then outline some special barriers women face in getting and using power.

First of all, in the new style organization, there are a large number of incentives for taking initiative beyond the bounds of the job and, in fact, that is what is expected. I am amused to hear that the Gannett Company has as its slogan for employees: "Do the right thing." That is the kind of slogan that Digital Equipment and Hewlett-Packard and Data General also give their people. They don't tell you how to do it; you can do anything you want, as long as it's the right thing. The fact is that an emphasis on entrepreneurial behavior and taking initiative beyond the bounds of the job can be very exciting but also often very frustrating.

Assignments in high tech organizations are often ambiguous. People are often given assignments that say nothing more than, "Solve the problem." In one large and prosperous conglomerate, a manager was told, "We've announced a new product to the public. Now make it happen." There are somewhat ambiguous assignments in which the result wanted is clearly spelled out but the means are left up to the individual.

Second, people are functioning in an environment in which there is a great deal of interdependence and overlap, perhaps multiple reporting relationships, four or five bosses, rather than a single boss. All of those articles now being written on "How to Manage Your Boss" should really say, in the high tech world, "How to Manage Your Bosses." In some ways, it is easier to manage your boss if there is more than one because that permits degrees of freedom, as in families when the children play parents off against one another. In the work situation, as in the family, one has alternatives if action is blocked in one direction. But overlap and interdependence also mean confusion about who has what territory. Many of these companies have an organization chart that looks like every other organization chart, but it will not tell you anything about how the work is actually done because of overlap and multiple connections. Third, there is a great deal of local autonomy in high tech companies, a great deal of freedom to invent and design new kinds of systems at a local level. In the high tech society, corporate headquarters may not be the scene of the action. It is in the division, the field operations, where things actually happen. The corporate staff members are often frustrated at designing and announcing policy that nobody in the field wants to accept since the emphasis is on providing as much local freedom as possible to stimulate initiative and innovation.

There is a culture of change in these organizations. Change is not a shock and a trauma; it is the fulfillment of an expectation that jobs will be changed frequently, people will move from job to job, there will be new inventions and new designs. It would be a failure for a manager in a high tech company to say, "All I did was perform my job very well." That is not an accomplishment. An accomplishment is inventing and designing something new. An accomplishment is being involved in change that increases the capacity of the organization.

There is also a culture of pride in those kinds of systems: that is one of the exciting things about working in high tech versus working in some of the matured and, some might say, failing industrial sectors. People feel not only proud of the success of an organization but proud of their own achievements. They say, "We're unique," "We're special," and "We hire only the best." When you, as an outsider, hear them say these things, it is somewhat distressing because you know they are no different from anybody else. But it is the case that, if you are being recruited by this kind of company, you will have as many as twenty face-to-face interviews before a decision is made. They have that kind of concern about selecting people who will fit their image of being the best and being special.

This culture of change and of pride makes people feel secure and valued enough to be willing to take some risks. The rewards come before the accomplishment, that is, not as a bonus at the end for having done something but the budget to do something interesting in the first place. As Tracy Kidder says in his Pulitzer Prize-winning book, *The Soul of a New Machine*, this kind of company and this kind of initiative within it is the wave of the future. It's like playing pinball: the reward is another game. You get to do it again and to' repeat the success.

This is a new and different world where power is more accessible at the local levels—power as information, resources, money, staff, space, time, and power as support, cooperation, backing, other people willing to be on one's team. Both kinds of power are more accessible in this kind of organization. One characteristic of a high tech society which shows that power is more easily attained is the pattern of rapid and open mobility. People move across and around the organization chart all over the place. By that I don't mean geographical mobility from one city to another, which may be important in some cases but is an artifact. High mobility within areas and across functions and around the system builds networks. That is one way networks are formed. One of your coworkers moves somewhere else in the system and you can go to him or her for something else.

Fourth, there is a great deal of employment security; that is important to look for. This is not to say that people have jobs for life but that people feel secure enough, certain enough that they will be here tomorrow, that they can take risks or join somebody's team or make a commitment to support a new idea. Organizations that are traumatized by change, where everybody fears who is going to be let go next, are not places where there is much power to be had or where it is easy to take the initiative and get something done.

There are many different professional and technical fields in a high tech organization, all interactive. People are not locked into their functional boxes. A system where each function talks only to itself and there is no interchange across professional or specialist boundaries promotes powerlessness. In these empowering new-style systems, team mechanisms, task forces, project teams, and special assignments pull people together across a wide variety of specialties; resources are decentralized, meaning that there are people right in your home office who have an extra bit in their budgets that you can tap. You don't have to go a thousand miles away or call long distance or put it over electronic mail to get what you need; it's there and available, locally.

Finally, in this high tech environment, it is possible to cut across the hierarchy to get what you need. I think this style of doing business will come to characterize all successful companies because it works. People are not bound by what has been traditional in American business. In the chain of command protocol, you had to ask your boss who asked his boss who asked his boss who asked her boss, and, if you were lucky, by the time your request got seven or eight layers up, somebody would listen. Or perhaps they were hoping that you would have gone away by the time your request made it up there. These new environments allow people to go directly, without stepping on anybody's toes or putting anybody's nose out of joint, to get what they need. It is a different world; it is more empowering but it also puts more burden on the individual to understand how to get and use power. If there is more potential in this kind of organization, there is also more frustration. You need to work through other people to get done what you need to get done. You can't do it alone. You can't rest on the authority of office to order other people to do what you want. You have to persuade them to join your team because they have other options. So an understanding of power becomes critical for survival in these sorts of organizations.

I like to use the word *power;* it is a strong word and I think we should use strong words rather than soft-pedal what really goes on. By power I do not mean domination or tyranny or control: that is the old hierarchical system of ordering people because of the force of the office. By power I mean the capacity to mobilize people, to get their cooperation, to get what you need to get the job done. It is power in the service of performance that is important and not power for its own sake. In fact, people who try to hoard power in organizations find that it disappears. It is not tangible; it is only the capacity to work to make something happen.

In a sense, much organizational power derives from reputation. You have it because other people are willing to let you have it and to help supply you with the tools you need to use it: information, resources, support, and backing. In new tech companies, power is not expressed in the trappings of office. Old style firms, as I wrote in *Men and Women of the Corporation,* put the most important people in the corner offices with the big windows. All you had to do was look at the draperies, the carpeting, and the number of ashtrays to know who was who in the pecking order. In the new tech firms, where the formal trappings of power have often disappeared, it takes more subtlety and sensitivity to figure out who really has it. Sometimes the whole company is in a converted old mill, or the powerful people are living in partitioned space where nobody can get privacy, or the boss is right down there in the cafeteria and has a middle office just like everybody else.

Identifying the ones who have power means identifying who gets invited to key meetings, who has to be checked with before you know a new policy will really work, who has been invited to be on task forces, whose signature or endorsement would really make a difference. When your colleague comes back from lunch to find a pile of phone messages on the desk, whose phone calls are returned first? That often says more about who has power than the boxes on the organizational chart or the formal symbols of status.

The powerless are the people who can easily be bypassed, left out. This has less to do with how well the technical part of the job is mastered and more to do with other organizational connections. The powerless, though competent, may be left out of critical decisions, bypassed in terms of their own authority. People might even say, "Don't bother, go over her head." Or the boss might say, if it is a woman and he feels he has done something dangerous by bringing her in, "Let me know how she's doing because I really want her to succeed." The hidden message is, "I'm concerned," and the image that one is powerless gets broadcast. Powerlessness also can come from not being in the know or in the functions that are close to the problem-solving, change-creating actions that the organization is now engaged in.

It is important to have power in the new tech organization; it is also important for any aspect of organizational leadership. A long tradition of research on leadership has found it very difficult to define who is a good leader on the basis of style or personal characteristics or even on the basis of situational determinants. What has turned out to be very important in defining leadership behavior and acceptance is power, clout, credibility. People prefer to work for bosses with power more than for bosses who practice good human relations or give a good performance appraisal. What good is praise without the organizational power to back it up and make something significant happen? Power has emerged as very important, a strong determinant of how well people actually function as leaders. The powerful get more cooperation more easily. There is evidence from many laboratory experiments as well as from field study of organizations to support this finding.

For example, there are experiments in which identical persons manage work groups. In one case they are presented as powerful, in the other as powerless. If the manager is thought to be powerful, he or she is responded to as effective, competent, wonderful to work with, bringing about high morale, and even, in some cases, as more attractive physically. (I call this the "Henry Kissinger syndrome.") The manager who is identified by the researcher as powerless is considered as less attractive and talking too much, gets more hostility expressed, receives less deference, and so forth. Remember this is exactly the same person, doing exactly the same things in the experiment.

Indeed, the powerful get so much cooperation so easily that they sometimes have to watch their casual hints or subtle suggestions because some zealous, ambitious young lieutenant may go out and implement them. (This is the "murder in the cathedral" problem: Henry the Second was casually saying to his aides, "I wish somebody would get rid of that pesky priest" and so they went out and murdered Thomas à Becket.) There are organizational war stories in the same genre. I visited some auto factories and was shown a whole section that looked odd. It turned out that the divisional general manager, a very powerful man, had visited one day and happened to admire some machinery painted green. So the word went out: "Hey, he likes green. Let's make everything green."

At the same time the powerless manage in the face of resistance. They are bypassed and undercut and left out of the action and their subordinates or peers feel, "I'll outlast them." "Why bother to cooperate with a powerless person?" This brings us to the negative consequences of powerlessness. I like to say that in organizations powerlessness corrupts. It creates petty tyrants rather than leaders. This accounts for lots of the stereotypes about women bosses and nagging housewives and old-maid schoolteachers. These are pictures of people who are powerless turning into petty tyrants because it is their only form of influence and control. When people won't respond to them, they start shouting and yelling. Sometimes the power-less look over other people's shoulders, breathing down their necks, not letting them have fun. "I'm not having any fun so I will use what control I do have to stop you from having fun." Sometimes they choose to reward mediocrity rather than rewarding talent.

There are bosses like that: powerless people in tenuous posi-tions who are threatened by anybody who might show them up. There is substantial research evidence suggesting that powerless peo-ple tend to be more rules-minded, focusing not on getting results but on behaving by the rules. In the high tech world, where there are very few rules and all that counts is results, powerless people hold themselves back and hold others back. Finally, the powerless become turf-minded, guarding their territory, trying to interfere with any-body else's productive action, playing king of the mountain. So powerlessness is a negative syndrome. You should want power not only to function well but because the lack of it makes us feel frus-trated, out of control, not respected, not listened to; it is just not a healthy way to function in an organization.

Power is accumulated two ways in an organization. The first way is through relationships, but I am not going to start with that because it is all too familiar to us. Those of you who read airline magazines will know that the image they present of people at work is that all they are doing is standing by the water cooler, plotting their next career moves and figuring out who to get to know. In fact, what most people do all day long at work is their job. The job and the kinds of activities that the job permits are the first real key to power. Jobs that help people accumulate power have a high component of discretion. In empowering jobs, there is a chance to invent, plan, create, design, even improve. The higher the component of routine, of established procedures, or of doing it the way the predecessor did, the more difficult it is to have power. Power tends to go to the pio-neers, the explorers of new territory, the first in a new function, rather than to the people who come later.

I have watched this happen in organizations. When a function is being designed in a new or critical area, the ones who line up to run that function are the people on the fast track. Sometimes they are known as the "water walkers" or "hot shots." (I collect those kinds of expressions. As the Eskimos have twenty-five words for snow,

American corporations have twenty-five words for rapidly upwardly mobile people. It shows what they are preoccupied with.) In one case, the water walkers all lined up to be the first to run that important and prestigious function. But when it came time to find a replacement, they had all disappeared. In fact—and this is a sad saga of organizational life—the job was downgraded under the second person.

This leads to dysfunctional games, of course. For example, the first thing a new manager does when coming in to take over a function is reorganize. Since the perfect organization hasn't been invented yet, there is probably some merit in reorganizing. But part of what that activity says is, "I'm going to emphasize the part I have invented, rather than the part that I have taken over from somebody else." It seems to me that if we had organizations that permitted that same creativity to be exercised in more productive ways, it would be better, but this is what people fall back on when they are looking for a place to stay and a way to put their personal stamp on a job.

So discretion is the first key characteristic. Power is, to some extent, operating at the edge of your competence. Power is operating in the realm you don't know yet. Powerless people start sharpening the pencils and falling back on routines at least they know they can do. But that only keeps them powerless.

A second activity that helps people gain power has to do with visibility. This is more than sending copies of every memo all over the organization, although popular career manuals often interpret visibility this way. In reality, jobs are differentially located with respect to the ability of the job holder to develop a track record. Visibility is partially dependent on physical location—headquarters versus boonies—but that is not always the critical factor. Digital Equipment, for example, has its own airline so people can easily move across facilities. Physical location is a little less important than it once was. But visibility is still important. It comes partly from having tangible results to show. That is in part what is important about sales. It isn't just the money, it is the tangibility of clear results, clearly measured. It is why people who do projects or define projects within the boundaries of a job get more attention. They can define "Time 1" when things were this way and "Time 2" where "I've moved or advanced over here."

The way a job is defined also helps provide power. Is it, for example, described as maintenance and support of ongoing routine or in terms of change, new developments, and new directions? Now, it is possible to use your discretion, to be noticed for it, and, at the same time, to be off the wall. Therefore, to have power in a job, you have to have the third criterion, which I call relevance. A relevant activity can be defined for this purpose as one which is oriented toward the organization's critical contingencies. Or, to put it another way, activities which are central to the resolution of external problems. The area that is outside the organization's control is going to be the hot area: what is pressing on the organization environmentally, the outside pressures from the economy, the government, and so on.

Power and uncertainty run in the same direction. The more uncertainty there is in a function—that is, the more unresolved questions, "things we don't know yet," the more dependence on parties out there making decisions that affect the organization—the more power the person who handles this function has.

One way to read the history of American business is to note that there was a time when most of the people who rose to the top and had power in large businesses were those who were in essential research and product development, the inventors. This still obtains in some high tech companies where the founder-inventor was the one who answered the first question: what are we going to invent to sell? But as that became routinized and the products were understood and under control, there was a wave of attention to the design engineers and the people who ran the manufacturing systems. Next, attention turned to sales and marketing, as in the late seventies when the auto industry noticed the Japanese competitors. Now attention seems to be turning to the financial and legal people, according to an article in the *Harvard Business Review*.[1] The economy is difficult; the functions of financial management and legal management become more pressing.

Sometimes young water walkers spend a good bit of time considering what job they should take next. Which will be the function where success is guaranteed? That is somewhat foolish because an organization needs everybody, even though some functions are

---

1. Robert H. Hayes and William J. Abernathy, "Managing Our Way to Economic Decline," *Harvard Business Review* 58,4 (July–August 1980): 67–77.

bound to be more powerful than others. The key is whether within a function it is possible to build relevance into activities rather than just doing them because they are traditional or because they are given. One finance department where I consult was astonished when I suggested that young accountants could actually go out and talk to their "customers." They could meet the people in the other departments they serve and ask them, "What do you need?" Every department can do that. Every function can try to tap into what is needed, what is necessary, what is relevant.

Taking these three characteristics of powerful jobs—discretion, visibility, and relevance—together, we can begin to understand the tradition that women have not had much power in organizations. One does not have to cite personal discrimination; one can see institutional patterns of women being tracked into jobs with less discretion, more routine, more orientation toward maintenance than to innovation, less visibility, and often no relevance to the hot areas. Women were in public relations and personnel, which, until recently, were not power centers in terms of the critical contingencies of the organization.

Now let's turn to the second way of accumulating power—other than through activities on the job—that is, through relationships. Having passed the water cooler, we now return to it. There are three logical possibilities for the kinds of relationships or alliances that build power: up, sideways, and down. (There is also outside, but we will leave that for a moment.) One finds sponsors, not in the sense of supporters but in the sense of people you can draw on to serve a critical function at a time when it is needed. This can be a key piece of information from somebody higher up, but that is all you go to that person for; maybe it is a letter of recommendation or an endorsement; perhaps it is the person who puts in a good word for you at a meeting you, as a junior person, can't attend.

These sponsors, or what used to be known as the "patronage system," are an important source of power. I say "sponsor" instead of "mentor" for a particular reason. In the 1950s women's magazines gave women two kinds of advice: how to dress and how to get a man. In the 1970s this advice changed to how to dress and how to get a mentor. It was essentially the same concept: "Mr. Right" in the office. Find him and your life is secure for all time. Now we know this is not true. So I prefer the concept of multiple sponsors—people who may not necessarily have a close relationship with you but who may write a key letter at the right moment or make a key phone call on your behalf.

One key to finding sponsorship is asking the sponsor to take only a limited risk. The sponsor does not have to endorse your total being and future career. He or she merely has to say, "Yes, on this project, I'll put in a good word." It also means never going to senior people to ask for sponsorship until you don't need it. You should not go until you have done so much homework and gotten so many other people to support it that you can take it to the sponsor and say something like, "These people are on board; I have done this search; I have this much data; this will really work." You minimize their risk. It is like getting a loan from a bank: it is much easier when you don't need it. One way to get sponsored is to operate independently, take initiative, and then go for sponsorship.

Having a powerful sponsor, however, is not enough. In high tech organizations, peers are important; they are the key to getting work done since territories overlap. There was a famous case recently where a woman was very competent and she had a powerful mentor. But she lost out because of having no peer relationships. Let me say one other thing about that case. It is sometimes said that the reason women have not succeeded in management is that we did not play football when we were twelve. Well, I played basketball and a lot of other team sports; I'm sure many of you did, too. The problem is *not* that we don't know how to play on teams. It is that it is very hard to play on a team that doesn't want you on it.

The third key to power through relationships is subordinates; it is downward in direction. It means not just subordinates but others junior to you, building your own team, grouping other people, passing on favors. Incidentally, in discussing mentors, nobody ever asks, "How do I be one?" I think we should be asking that question. We cannot just consider ourselves and our own lives; we owe it to one another to help one another. George Gilder says selfish greed motivates all of us. Even on that basis, we can say that we can do better individually if the whole organization goes well. There is surely some virtue in making sure that others are empowered as we go along.

Gaining power through relationships has been a little more difficult for women than for men, not because we don't have the skills but because there have been an awful lot of them and very few of us. Although I tout the value of high technology companies, there are still women suffering from isolation and neglect, even in those companies. There are cycles of advantage and cycles of disadvantage. Powerlessness is part of the cycle of disadvantage that people get caught in. Powerlessness breeds less effective leadership, people who are too controlling, too rules-oriented, and it fosters low morale. That just keeps them powerless. It is a cycle that keeps building. What we want is more power for our own success and for the success of our organizations. With the economy in the shape that it is in, we should all be pulling for American business. Power breeds effective leadership and that produces more power. That is really what I want to leave you with: more power.

Discussion

The lone worker who differs from the majority in a work group by age or sex or race does indeed feel alone, because he or she is treated differently and perceived differently than the others are. How such "O's" in an "X" world can help themselves was the theme of several questions.[2] Professor Kanter reiterated the importance of networks by citing the example of one of the top corporate women in America who uses Kanter's consulting firm, an advertising agency with a key woman executive, and a search firm that is headed and run by a woman. "I don't believe she has ever said a word about seeking to use all these female vendors." Instead, Kanter reported, she just brought them in because they could do the job. The ladies' room near her office is awfully crowded, Kanter said.

Kanter outlined two strategies for "getting more O's in:" inside and outside. The outside strategy is activism. It involves keeping alive the notion that it is an important thing to do. We need to support the women's movement organizations, she said, even if one might not want to have that commitment known on the job. Part of the sadness of the failure of the Equal Rights Amendment, Kanter said, is that women as a group must show that they care about it, that they are a political force, and that they cannot be ignored. Even the most strident activists are doing all women a favor, she said. Another effective outside strategy, being pursued by women in great numbers, is to get the education and credentials we need.

Personal, or inside, strategies should be subtle. Don't say, "I want more women in that department so I am going to bring in five women candidates;" just continue to bring in names of excellent women candidates. When you are in a position to bring people in or give people visibility, make sure that at least a good proportion of them are women. You don't want to overdo it, but it is good to talk up women and women's achievements. If you circulate an article around your office about the technical end of your business, find one by a woman. Make women visible as visitors, as speakers. We can't advocate knee-jerk support of all women just because they are

---

2. "The Tale of O," a tape and slide presentation by Rosabeth Moss Kanter, is copyrighted by Goodmeasure, Inc., Cambridge, Massachusetts.

women, but criticism of women is often translated, "Well, if even women don't want her. . . ." If you see a woman who is not doing well, you might want to work it out with her privately rather than gossip about her.

One questioner asked how an "O" could cope with being under a powerless boss. Kanter suggested that she could build peer relationships and try, at the same time, to get out from under. It is good to have other people in the organization know what you are doing. The worst thing a powerless boss can do to a subordinate is to be the sole information source about her, her sole link with the rest of the organization. Another possibility is to consider what she can do to lessen her boss's powerlessness, how she can help him look good. A good source of information is an article in the February 1981 issue of *Ms.* magazine. A source of technical material on organizational studies, Kanter said, is the *Administrative Science Quarterly*, an authoritative journal in the field.

On the issue of appearance—an "O" dressing to look like an "X"—Kanter held that one has to be true to oneself. We have to, insofar as possible without doing damage to our personal integrity, honor the culture that is out there, but there may be times when we say, "We don't have to be that way" or "We don't have to do it that way."

One rule of thumb is that professional relationships should be professional. We should strive to be task oriented. This may mean carrying not only the trappings but the behaviors of the task-oriented. The reason that the X's and the O get together is to get the job done, Kanter said. Is the informal kidding around and the informal relationship all that important? Some people put their jackets on when they get down to real work, she said. "I never take my jacket off," she remarked. On the other hand you don't have to stop being a person. There are still good people out there, even if it is said to be a jungle. Perhaps the best advice, she concluded, is to remain professional at all times, maybe even a little more professional than the X's. You shouldn't let your personal characteristics intrude too much, she said. We don't really have to talk about last weekend's ball game, Kanter said. There are subjects such as travel, which are part of the shared culture. Kanter recounted a recent meeting with two new business contacts who, like her, turned out to have three-year-olds.

On the way from the airport, they had an interesting discussion about pediatricians, toilet training, and child care. Kanter cited that to show that there is a new culture. There are lots of vestiges of the old but there are also glimmerings of a new world coming.

New women bosses are often criticized, and their performance is cited as evidence that women cannot be good bosses. Kanter attributed that in part to the fact that women are still, by and large, inexperienced. Women may still have to live up to a higher standard than men do. That may continue, Kanter said, until we have a critical mass. Then individual women will not have to be seen as representing their whole sex. She noted that at Yale University there are noncredit courses in communications, making presentations, and writing, which help men and women start the management programs at the same place. Once we have a critical mass, she said, then we can all be, not O's, but individuals again.

Being a Manager in a Multicultural World

Pam McAllister Johnson

On a recent business trip, I read a magazine article entitled, "That's No Lady, That's My Boss." The first sentence asked, "What's more difficult than having a woman boss?" The answer was simple: being one. From my experience as the first black woman newspaper publisher in the United States, I can tell you that is true.

As a woman executive, you have to be careful not to let others define you because they may, too often, define you in negative terms. In order to be a successful executive, you have to have strong feelings of self worth. It is especially important not to define yourself solely in terms of your job. Too many people over whom you have too little control can have a negative impact on you and your job.

A second important point is that you cannot be afraid of your own aggression or of getting angry. Sometimes women managers

---

Pam McAllister Johnson is publisher of the *Ithaca* (NY) *Journal*, a post she has held since 1981. She holds three degrees from the University of Wisconsin: the B.S. in journalism (1967), the M.A. in journalism and educational policy (1971), and the Ph.D. in mass communications and educational psychology (1977). Johnson has taught at Norfolk State University, the University of Missouri, and the University of Wisconsin. She has served as a researcher and reporter for CBS Network News, Chicago Bureau, as a reporter for educational television and radio, and has had extensive experience in news reporting for print media.

spend an inordinate amount of time worrying about hurting or alienating subordinates. A psychologist put it well when she said, "Aggression that turns into a pathological need to dominate, control, or hurt others is well worth avoiding. Yet . . . a fear of one's own healthy aggression causes serious problems." Sometimes we have to be aggressive to bring about changes. But we have to learn to use our anger and our aggression constructively.

The corporation I work for has a slogan: "Do the right thing." When I first heard that, I said, "You have got to be kidding." I could not believe that such a complex organization would have such a simplistic slogan. But people in my organization really do give one another that advice. Somebody says, "Hey, I've got a problem. What do you think I should do about it?" Some executive is likely to answer, "Do the right thing." And there is something to it. We have to look for solutions to problems in terms of what is right for the business and for us as individuals.

Affirmative action as a moral persuasion has not been as effective as we had hoped it would be. Some people thought it took advantages away from them, rather than helping them to win the game. We have to let business people know that we are in as game players. We are in there to help them win—and we can help them win.

A social researcher, Daniel Yankelovich, has recently classified American workers into five groups: (1) the "Go Getters," the young and ambitious: 15 percent; (2) the "Work before Pleasure," older, more dedicated ones: 19 percent; (3) the "Habitual Workers," older, blue-collar job holders: 22 percent; (4) the "Middle Managers," young, educated: 17 percent; and (5) the "Turned Off," poorly educated, low income: 27 percent.[1] This may not be a definitive classification, but it is interesting to see where you fit. I suspect that this change in the diversity of the work force may call for a more diverse management style. Research indicates that the better the management style, the higher the productivity. High productivity means high profits. It means winning the game. The multicultural manager

---

1. Daniel Yankelovich, *New Rules: Searching for Self-Fulfillment in a World Turned Upside Down* (New York: Random House, 1981).

realizes the full diversity of society and is able to interact professionally with people who are different. People constantly ask me what it is like to be black and a woman. Facetiously I reply, "I've been black for thirty-six years and a woman for thirty-six years and I have no problem with it." I try to explain how I feel about my "differences" by sharing the following anecdote. My first job as a journalist fifteen years ago was as a reporter for the *Chicago Tribune*. I found myself spending 75 percent of my time convincing my colleagues that it was all right for me to be black, a female, and a reporter. I found I was letting others define and place me in a handicapped position so I reversed the percentages—25 percent answering those questions and 75 percent being what I was hired to be, a good reporter.

By force or by choice, black Americans are multicultural. We have to be able to function in more than one community. Unfortunately, that ability is not particularly valued. I also think it is more difficult for white people to be multicultural than for blacks. For example, when black people are successful, others say, "Ah, yes, they learned the game, they are assimilated, they are all right." But a white person who is multicultural is labeled a "hippie" or an eccentric or a liberal. Labels are difficult to live with. What we all want is to be treated as individuals.

When I define myself as a black woman, I define those characteristics as positives, not as handicaps. I tell employers that I bring a larger perspective to the job than other candidates might. I have a strong and diverse educational, professional, and social background. How many publishers have Ph.D.'s in mass communications? How many publishers have worked for top print and broadcast companies? How many publishers have been totally immersed in different ethnic cultures? I have dealt with a more di verse group of people in more diverse situations than most. I went to an all-black elementary school, a Jewish junior high school, and a black high school. I had friends who were on welfare; I had some friends who were wealthy. I could feel comfortable with both of them because I define myself. So I would say to you that I hope you can define yourself in strong, positive statements and actions.

Coping with Illegal Sex Discrimination

Linda Bartlett

We can accept certain things as given for this presentation. First, there are laws in the United States that say an employer cannot discriminate against a worker on the basis of sex, race, religion, or national origin. Second, there are federal agencies, such as the Equal Employment Opportunity Commission, to deal with complaints of illegal employment discrimination. Third, the states each have their agencies—in New York, it is the Human Rights Commission. There are also city agencies: New York City has a Human Resources Division, which handles discrimination complaints.

Our discussion today assumes that you have been hired. That is no small thing. It used to be the case that women could not be hired above the clerical level in big corporations. But now, we can. The staff positions are easier to get than the line jobs, but at least now we can get in.

Linda Bartlett has been associate general counsel of the Directors Guild of America, Inc., since 1981. She earned the B.A. in mathematics and economics in 1964 from Brooklyn College, did graduate work in economics at the City University of New York, and earned the J.D. degree *cum laude* from the University of Miami School of Law, Coral Gables, in 1977. Her postgraduate experience includes service as an attorney with Benjamin Wyle, Esq., of New York City in labor law and commercial practice and with Klecan and Roach, P.S., Albuquerque, New Mexico, in trial and appellate practices in all phases of civil litigation and settlement.

But we must not rest on our laurels because, as many women are finding today, there is still discrimination; there is still fierce resistance to the promotion of women. Nobody says anymore, "You can't have this job because you are a black" or "We won't hire you because you are a woman." My first employer asked me, could I type? Who would be taking care of my children? Would I be worrying about them all the time? Employers can no longer legally ask these questions, but they can wonder. Perhaps they have wives who stay home and take care of children. They know their wives are doing full-time jobs. They may not understand how a woman can be a responsible worker and still be a parent. This puts the burden on us. We have to be able to say, "Look, I made it through three years of law school; I can surely make it through the three months' probation period here." We have to reassure the employer that we won't want our children to be neglected or to be suffering at home alone. Of course we will make provision for them. I think we should recognize his concerns as legitimate, even though a male single parent, with exactly the same burdens, won't have any trouble assuring the boss that he will be responsible.

The law requires that the employer who needs something moved from here to there has absolutely no right to take a look to see if the hand is a woman's hand or a black hand, a man's hand or an Hispanic hand. If the person can do the job, the employer cannot take these other characteristics into account. Supposing an employer does take those characteristics into account and does make decisions about salary or promotion or work assignment on the basis of those characteristics. I cannot stress enough that you should try to resolve the problem within the organization without using the legal route. You should try every available avenue inside the organization before you file suit. The legal route is not a satisfactory one; even if you win a case, you will have lost because of the stress involved in litigation. There are times when there is no other recourse, but you had better be absolutely certain.

Big corporations have affirmative action officers or equal opportunity officers. These are people who supposedly understand the law and are supposed to be sympathetic to your claims. You must go to them first, for two reasons. First, it might resolve the problem. Second, if it doesn't solve it and you have to take your claim further, at least the company is on notice that these problems exist. That will be an important part of your proof. When you have some evidence that something illegal is going on, don't wait until you get embroiled in a big dispute. Go to the affirmative action people and lay out the problem. If there is a union, it will often have staff who can help you.

There are many types of sexual harassment. Sometimes you can handle it yourself by just saying, "Look, fella, this really bothers me." Take account of his feelings by saying something on the order of, "I don't think you mean to insult me," but then say it straight, "This really bothers me so could you just cool it." Sometimes that works; sometimes it doesn't.

Take a case of suspected sex discrimination of another kind. Suppose you have been in a staff manager's position for about four years. You have worked hard; you have been given good reviews and decent salary increments. Then your boss's job opens up. You are in line for it in terms of seniority and experience, but you don't get it. Or let's say you get it, but at half the pay of your male predecessor. Or take another situation. You apply for this position and you get to see Jim, who is in charge of filling it. He says, "I'd really like to discuss this with you but I don't have much time. Could we meet at seven for dinner?" You say you are sorry but you are busy. He says, "How about tomorrow night?" You say you are sorry but you are busy then, too. He says, "Well, I just won't be able to see you for ten days. Come back then." And, within a week, the position is filled.

These are all actionable claims of sex discrimination. The sex of the candidate is affecting the management decision about who is to fill the job at what salary. There has been progress in hiring, but much less progress where promotions are concerned.

Women are not too welcome in boardrooms yet. One excuse sometimes used is that they don't have two bathrooms. It was a real shock to me to walk into a judge's chambers and ask if I could please take care of my needs and be told, "I don't believe you'll find a ladies' room." So I said to the judge, "I know your honor has a private bathroom. Would it be all right if I used that?" No, no. There was an uproar until somebody realized that the jury room attached to the chambers had a bathroom. No ladies' room in the boardroom.

I would advise you not to ignore instances of discrimination.

Suppose your boss, your immediate supervisor, keeps saying, "Come on out to lunch with me" or he just outright propositions you. I wouldn't just say no and let it ride. He will get back at you later. Then when you don't get something you deserve and you say you are being discriminated against because you would not sleep with the boss, higher management may well say, "Why didn't you come to us immediately?"

It is important to keep careful records. You make it easier for the people in labor relations to help if you have records of what happened. To say, "He bothered me many times" or "I have been unfairly passed over for promotion over and over" is not nearly so useful as being able to tell the exact nature of the incidents—what dates, who was present, what was said, what exactly were the job openings in question, what were the qualifications of the people who got them, what exactly was told to you as the reasons you didn't get them, by whom, when, and where. When the thing comes to a head, you will be emotional. It is extremely helpful to have documentation. In a roomful of smoke, it is hard to find the handles on the fire doors.

Throughout all of this, of course, you have to be sensible. If you take a discrimination problem to your supervisor, you are going to create tensions at work. If you call somebody on something, he is going to be angry. Eventually, everybody in the whole place may know that you are the one who claimed sexual harassment or discrimination in promotions or whatever it was. "Look at her," some people will say. "She thinks she should have gotten that job. What a joke! She's only been here thirteen years." You end up being blamed for fighting discrimination.

As you well know, the victim in a rape case often is treated as the perpetrator. "You asked for it, didn't you?" "Why were you wearing that short dress?" Nobody will ask the banker why he had such a big wad of money in his pocket for somebody to pick, but they will surely ask about dress length in a rape trial.

We should be prepared to have it said that we who complain about discrimination are just opportunists, that we are using the existence of those laws as a way of getting ahead. We have to steady ourselves beforehand, knowing our motives will be questioned. We must be prepared for tactics management people will use to defend themselves. If you go to an agency to complain about being passed over for promotion, the employer may respond to the charge by saying, "Hey, I didn't know she wanted that job." So document the fact that you applied and be prepared to give evidence that you are qualified. The ultimate weapon at our disposal is that we can group together in class action suits. Companies usually make effective and affirmative changes when faced with financial liability and injunctive relief in these actions.

My final piece of advice on resolving problems at work is this one. If you become a manager—and not everyone in this room will—I urge you not to forget your roots. Tomorrow, when you have made it, remember the fears you have today. Try very hard to understand the people over whose lives you have control at work. Don't ever forget.

The Single Woman: Moving Up by Moving Around

Carol Kiryluk

All of you know the single woman: she is the one thought to have all the time in the world because she has no "responsibilities." I thought I would tell you a bit about life in a corporation from the vantage point of a single woman today. First, the fact that I am single has never seemed to me to be the central fact about me. It is true that I have always thought in terms of a career but not true that I have ever consciously said, "If I want a responsible job, I can't get married." There are costs to every benefit, and I'll admit to having chalked off a few in my eleven plus years in employee relations. I'll admit to routinely putting in twelve- to fourteen-hour days; having been transferred seven times in the last eleven years, back and forth among five different cities; traveling and working weekends and going to meetings scheduled after 5 p.m. as a matter of course—much

Carol Kiryluk has been manager of career development, staffing, and equal employment opportunity of the exploration and producing division of the Mobil Corporation, New York City, since February 1982. Prior to that, Kiryluk was staff assistant in employee relations and in labor relations, employee relations manager, career development and staff services manager, and regional recruiting coordinator, all at divisions of Mobil in Chicago, Dallas, Los Angeles, and at corporate headquarters. She earned the B.S. in sociology at the University of Pennsylvania (1968) and the Master of Industrial and Labor Relations at Cornell University (1970).

of which does not accommodate an active social life. But it has been my choice.

I have noticed that people presume that a move is easier on a single person than on an employee with a family. It is assumed, somehow, that a single person can be moved without problems: he or she has nobody else to be responsible for and no one else's adjustment to worry about. At the same time, the single person has no one else to deal with the disposition of a residence, to haggle with the packers, or to be a portable support system. The fact is that every move brings about disorientation and a need for reorientation. It is certainly no easier when you are doing it alone.

I recently transferred back to New York from an assignment in Texas, and I made a key decision: to be more permanently in one place, at least for a few years. There may, however, be compelling professional or personal reasons that will require me to pack up again and start over in a new city, find a new apartment, find new friends, cope with moving the pets and the plants and the telephone and the subscriptions and all the rest of it. When that time comes, I'll do it.

Making a decision to move or not has career consequences. When one is being moved about, it is not on a whim. One tries to get exposure and experience in as many areas as possible. Maybe you change location to be able to move from a staff assistant position to your first supervisory job. If, for example, you are in human resources or personnel, you will find that most departments are small. It is very unlikely that you can move into your boss's job; to move up, you may have to go somewhere else. My history has been that of moving between units to pick up more experience, more responsibility, more risk, different perspectives. It has been exciting, but each time I have moved I have found it an increasingly tough battle to maintain personal balance and my sense of self. The temptation has been to throw myself into the job to prove to everybody that I was the most competent person around. It is easy not to take the time to look at the number of hours you are putting in and the price you are having to pay in terms of giving up life off the job.

I think you are in trouble if you find you can't discuss your work problems really frankly with anyone because you have no real friends outside your work circle. That is too solitary and lonely. A problem faced by women who are moved around a lot is that they feel they have to reprove themselves in each new work situation. Women have to deal with an environment where women in management may or may not be something new. You are moved to a new office; the men there may be older than you are and they may not be terribly excited at the prospect of reporting to you. They may never like you but if they are tuned in, they will realize that you can offer them opportunities that they would not have if you were not their supervisor. And, in the long run, it is not a matter of choice. They have to deal with your being there and likely accept it because you have been sent there for a purpose: to get the job done. I find it is helpful to focus on the job to be done and to try not to get caught up in worrying about whether or not my subordinates or coworkers think I am nice. It is not a popularity contest.

Perhaps the most important thing is to develop one's life outside the work situation. You need the balance of satisfactions outside the office and things to look forward to other than triumphs at work. The problem is that when you suffer some reversal at work, where there is some personal project that goes wrong, you cannot turn to a support system the way married people can.

In a new environment, it is essential to find somebody to talk with. You need to strategize, to take stock, to put the hassles in perspective. It is best to find somebody outside your work to talk to who is neutral to the situation. When looking things over, you may find you are dealing with a general problem others are experiencing—you are not alone. Or you may find that what you are experiencing doesn't have anything to do with you as an individual, personally. At times all you need is someone to help put things in perspective.

Betty Lehan Harragan spoke about the role of the mentor. I have found it helpful to be able to speak to people more senior than I in the company and I am comfortable going to ask for advice. It doesn't just fall into your lap; you have to ask for it. Nor should you expect—or want—constant feedback. But there are people you can trust for objective counsel.

There are opportunities for women like you and me in "classical" staff functions. Since the economy is scaling down and manpower utilization is a critical issue, human resource management is becoming more and more important. It is too bad that has to be the reason but there it is. The fact is that many corporations are scaling down. Key advisors in personnel utilization are employee relations people. So there are opportunities for women who are willing to take on hard jobs and contribute to tough decisions.

For my part, I have found it is exciting to take a step every now and then outside of a comfortable environment. It is scary to the point that, later, you may look back and wonder where you found the courage. But you did and that is satisfying. I would like to encourage those of you who are in support areas and to remind you that there is a future for you. There are even roads to line management. To be sure, it is very competitive. But the best way to travel those roads is to be the best equipped person you can be in terms of education and experience and to do your best to keep a balanced perspective.

Dual Career Couples:
How the Company Can Help

Eleanor Byrnes

A company like my bank is interested in dual career couples. I would like to begin my presentation by saying why that should be so. Second, I will describe what we are doing to help resolve some of the problems professional couples face—probably the shortest part of my talk. And third, I want to talk about the challenges that lie ahead, which will no doubt be the longest part.

I think that many corporations share the philosophy that it makes good business sense to hire women. Recruiting and hiring large numbers of qualified women has not proven to be a problem for us: our training program has between forty and fifty percent women. Women have, of course, been in financial service industries longer than they have been in other kinds of industrial and manufacturing organizations as managers, so it has perhaps been easier for us than for others. Eli Ginzberg of Columbia University has predicted

Eleanor Byrnes has been with the Continental Illinois National Bank and Trust Company of Chicago since 1977. She earned the B.A. degree from Connecticut College in 1968; the M.A. in teaching from Boston College in 1970; and a Middle Management Certificate from Simmons College in 1979. Initially in corporate planning at Continental Bank, Byrnes moved to the personnel department in 1978, where her responsibilities included professional placement that year, college relations in 1979, and currently, internal placement. Her title is personnel officer.

that, of the new entrants into the work force in the 1980s, two-thirds will be women. Of those, half will have college degrees. So it makes sense to be interested in developing and retaining good women.

Over the past five years in our bank, we have hired many good women with M.B.A. degrees, and they have proven to be good investments. Many are now married; they want to start their families. We have put a lot of money into these people; they have been successful; we do not want to lose them.

What are we doing to make it possible for women and men to have both serious careers and family lives? First, this year, as our bank celebrates its one hundred twenty-fifth anniversary, we are beginning to hire relatives of people already working for us. We have gotten rid of a nepotism rule we have had for all these years.

A second step we have taken is to join with other organizations in Chicago to form a spouse employment network. If we hire a person who is married to a professional, we offer to help the spouse find work by referring the resume to our network. Fifteen of the largest employers in Chicago have agreed to be part of this network; all have agreed to give spouses' resumes a good hard look—not just stamp it, as we say, with the old silver bullet.

Beyond that, we are committed by company practice to helping dual career couples not lose anything if we transfer one of the partners. Our problem is that we have opened many new branches around the country and overseas and we need to staff them in a logical and efficient manner. When the person we transfer is married to a professional, we hire outside consultants to help the spouse find work in the new place. The message we give our people is that we do not want a transfer to disrupt a spouse's career. We try very hard to get her (it is usually her, but we have had two hims so far) a new opportunity in the new location. The consultant helps put the resume together, targets companies in the new city, and assists in the whole job search process.

We also have a maternity leave coordinator in our personnel department. Actually, we would like to call this person "child care leave coordinator," but some feel we shouldn't until at least one man asks for child care leave. This person assists professional and executive-level women to arrange for maternity leave. Our current policy is that the mother combines disability leave with six months of unpaid maternity leave. The maternity leave coordinator assists the returning staff woman to go back to her old job or locate another. If she wants to go on part time or flextime, the maternity leave coordinator helps her to do that.

One woman for whom these practices are working neatly is a lending officer in Denver. She had her first baby this year; her boss moved a terminal into her home; she works from the terminal now. When her maternity leave is up, she is coming back full time to the bank. We have another lending officer whose beat was Marakesh. When she had a baby, she decided she did not want to travel those distances for a while so she transferred to a part-time job in our public affairs area, where she is developing another of her interests, the fine arts. She is home part time because, as she says, there is no instant replay of the growing years and she doesn't want to miss it all.

When I got back from maternity leave, a year and a half ago, I tried to find a way to get together with others who had or were having the same experiences I was having. When I was pregnant, I felt that I was making many of the men managers uncomfortable. So we had "Women and Work" seminars at which some of us could get together and talk. Our first topic was our feelings when we found out that we were pregnant. The consensus was that we all felt guilty. "How am I going to tell my manager? I just got into this new job." It seemed sad to us that we had felt guilty about one of the nicest things that ever happened to us. We discussed how one can talk to one's manager about being pregnant and how to handle the assumption that you don't want to travel when you are pregnant and so on.

Now we have branched out: we have a consulting psychologist from Northwestern Medical School who comes to meet with two different groups. One is for women like me who are trying to handle the juggling act of career and children. The other group, which is a little more daring and secretive, is for women who are considering having children.

Also, as I have mentioned, we have a strong internal placement network. One problem we are still wrestling with is the belief that lending cannot be done on a part-time basis yet. Managers feel that our bank will be at a disadvantage if we assign a customer a part-time person while a competitor offers him or her a full-time officer.

Our returnees have different kinds of constraints: some can't travel now, which limits them because international and multinational jobs just require travel; in fact, some domestic jobs do, too. The internal placement unit helps to identify a position that will use the person's skills but still pay attention to the limitations.

What are the challenges ahead at corporations like ours? One problem is that our *top* managerial ranks are still composed only of men and virtually all men from traditional families, that is, they have what we call "enabling wives"—wives who support them and enable them to do what they have to to be successful. When one of our young women managers gets pregnant, the older managers tend to say, "Ah, you can't count on those women. You can't plan around them." In a way, that is true. We can't plan around them but we can surely try our best to keep them and help them when their children are little. We try to educate these senior managers by telling them about our successes.

Our managers also need a little re-education on the matter of mobility. It is not as easy to move people around as it once was—spouses' careers and children's educations get in the way. We have to learn to respond to these concerns: to make it easier for people to move or, if they won't, to not hold it against them and to make sure they are offered other opportunities.

Another stumbling block we have is our benefits package. Ours, like that at many another corporation, is still geared to the traditional family: medical insurance, life insurance, x number of vacation days, disability insurance. The dual career family is looking for a more flexible cafeteria style of benefits, where one partner whose spouse got enough coverage in one area could trade that one in for something that would fill his or her needs better.

Finally, there is the challenge of child care. Corporations are, as you know, leery of getting involved; they want to leave that responsibility to individuals. However, my bank is talking with other Chicago employers about the possibility of setting up a corporate-sponsored child care center jointly with the YWCA. This is just at the talking stage now; I hope it will be a reality.

In summary, I see new values emerging in some corporations today. There are people who care very much about having a separate life and career, people whose careers and whose family lives are both very important to them. They feel strongly that their work should not take over their whole lives, leaving only a little piece of time for their families. These people are high productivity people; they are making a serious commitment to their jobs but one that has, as it should for everybody, limits. That distinction is one to which corporations ought to pay attention.

Working Couples and Child Care

Patricia M. Oesterle

The first thing to consider in choosing among different kinds of child care is how much time you and your husband are prepared to devote to taking care of your child. Half-time? Two-thirds time? Is it possible to arrange work for either of you in that way? A second consideration is where each of you is in your career development. We go through stages in our careers; sometimes it is more convenient for one or the other to take on more responsibility, to be the primary care-giver, even if there is some other kind of care involved as well. One of you will have to stay home when the child is sick. That can depend on where each of you is in the career cycle.

Other factors to consider are the number of children you plan altogether and your own personal values about child rearing. Do

Patricia M. Oesterle is an attorney in private practice in Ithaca, New York, where her specialties include family law, real estate, litigation, estate planning, and business law. Oesterle earned the B.A. with distinction and high honors in psychology at the University of Michigan in 1972 and the J.D. from Wayne State University Law School in 1975, where she was a member of the law review. Her legal experiences includes serving as a law clerk for Gregory, Van Lopik and Higle, Detroit; as law clerk to the Honorable Ross W. Campbell, Circuit Judge in Ann Arbor, and as an Associate with Smart & Associates, P.C., Richmond, Virginia, where her areas of practice included representation of builders, developers, buyers, and sellers of residential and commercial property, estate planning, general business law, and family law.

you think it is essential that the child be in your home, with one of you? If you are willing to consider other settings part of the time, do you prefer group care or family care? I am told that, in the old days, a working mother could turn to her own mother or mother-in-law for child care. Well, that is not so anymore. Women in that generation are out working.

First, let me talk about options for preschool children. The most ideal, in my opinion, is to have live-in help. The advantages are obvious: no worry about times when you get home late, no worry about sickness, no problems with car pools. You might even find someone who will prepare dinner, do light housekeeping, run errands, do grocery shopping, and so on. If you have more than one child, this can be less expensive than making arrangements for outside care for two or three. But the disadvantage of live-in help is that it is expensive. Even though there are two earners in the family, you still have to make a fair amount to be able to afford live-in help, even for five working days, never mind the weekend. Another possibility is an *au pair*, a visitor from another country, but there is the problem of limited visas.

The next most realistic option is family day care: you take your child to someone else's home, where the care-giver has a small group of children ranging in age from two to ten years old. This costs between $30 and $45 a week (in contrast to $4 or $5 an hour, plus benefits, for live-in help). You need to be selective when you choose family day care: some are very good; others, not so good, relying, in my opinion, on putting the children in front of television far too much of the day. It is good to have a clear understanding with the care-giver on advance notice for days off and vacation. Family care-givers often will not accept children under two years old.

A third possibility is institutional day care, which usually does not accept children under three, sometimes two. In Ithaca, there is a wide range of nursery schools—structured, unstructured, regular menu, vegetarian. These schools usually have hours from about 7:30 a.m. to 5:30 p.m., which can be a problem when you have late meetings. Another disadvantage of institutional care is that the center may be understandably picky about taking your child if he or she is a little bit sick.

Once your children are in school, your problems narrow (or

expand, depending on how you look at it) to the hours after school, what to do on snow days and holidays, how to cope when the children are sick, and how to handle the summer. Once the children are school age, there are also lessons and clubs and meetings, not to mention visits to the doctor, the dentist, and the orthodontist. This takes an incredible amount of organization and juggling.

If you are the parent who cuts back on work to part time, you should be prepared for the fact that most of your salary goes to child care for the time you do work. You may not even break even for a couple of years but you are keeping your career on line. There are disadvantages: you have to keep organizing and reorganizing the child care arrangements. Sometimes there is stress at work and you come home and there's a mess, too. The baby-sitter needs time off the next day; you have an important meeting scheduled; your husband does, too. So you have to make some compromise somewhere.

Sometimes I think that many of us try to be superwomen: to have immaculate homes, lovely children humming as they go about their daily tasks in their intellectually stimulating, super-progressive day care setting, and super success at ever-increasing responsibilities at work. Somewhere along the line, we have to give ourselves permission to be less than perfect. Just having children slows down careers. How much you will be slowed depends on your occupation but this is a reality and should be faced.

When I was in law school, I thought there was only one way to become successful: one lock-step career ladder I could climb. Everybody wanted to do the same thing. But I have come to realize that life is not that simple. We are going to have long lives; we can build in a lot of flexibility if we want to. I started practicing law when I was twenty-four, so I figure I have a span of 40 to 45 years of total practice. I figure I can gear down in these years to take care of my two and a half year old. My career may not move as fast as it would have but now I have the child I wanted very much. I have found it very personally satisfying to be able to have both a career and a family. I hope you do, too.

Does Becoming a Parent Mean Falling Off the Fast Track?

Gail Bryant Osterman

Let me tell you about a typical working day for a professional couple with a preschool child. They live in the suburbs; he commutes about twenty-five minutes to his office; she commutes over one hour each way to Manhattan by train. They have a two-year-old daughter who attends a preschool center a couple of blocks from home.

The day starts early. The mother gets up at 5:00, takes a shower, gets dressed, and wakes up her daughter at 5:30. Sometimes the daughter is already awake; she knows the schedule. The mother and daughter have an hour alone together for games, songs, and stories; at 6:30, they wake the man of the house. After a few minutes, the mother kisses them both good-bye and walks to the station to catch the train at 6:47. She has to be in the office at 8:15; she allows an extra quarter of an hour for train delays and often needs it.

Meantime, back at home, the father and daughter get dressed, make breakfast, and make some attempt at straightening the house.

Gail Bryant Osterman earned the Bachelor of Fine Arts at Stephens College in 1971 and the Master of Science at Cornell University in 1976. Since 1976, she has been in the field of international marketing. At the time of this conference, Osterman was employed by a major U.S. corporation as an export sales specialist with responsibility for sales, promotion, and trademark protection of corporate names in the international market. Osterman lives with her husband and child in Westchester County, New York.

If it is Thursday, they leave a special list of instructions for the cleaning service before they leave for the preschool center. Once there, the father has to greet the pet guinea pigs, get the daughter's coat off and get her settled, and have a few words with the teachers. By this time, it is 8:30 and time for him to go to work. If they are lucky, the day will go smoothly for all three. Some sacrifice of sleep has given the mother time to be with her daughter; the father and daughter have a special relationship because of their time together in the morning. The daughter particularly enjoys making the all-important decision of what to have for breakfast. Equally important for this family is the child's enrollment in a quality preschool center, which is a popular one with a long waiting list. It is also expensive.

In the evening of this typical day, the process is reversed. The schedule requires that both parents leave work on time to avoid complications. The father has to pick up his daughter before the center closes at 5:30, after which they do errands—go to the dry cleaner and such—before they go to the train station to pick up the mother. Making dinner is a family activity, as is cleaning up afterwards. Then comes a bath for the daughter, and story time for her, and then bedtime for her at 9:00. Then the parents sit down together unless the father has one of the professional meetings which characterize his profession, about once or twice a week.

This is a normal day. It sounds routine, automatic, and as simple as one, two, three. But with the pressure, tension, stress, fatigue, and isolation of this kind of life, it is a pressure-cooker existence. It means sixteen hours of a fast-paced, nonstop schedule for the mother; a few hours more or less, depending on his evening schedule, for the father. Their life is all work and family. There is barely time to sit down, never mind time for friends or personal hobbies.

And this working woman is lucky. Her husband shares equally in the family and household responsibilities. Unlike many working couples, they do not have to worry about finding quality child care; for the present, they have found it. They can manage it financially— both the child care and the household cleaning service.

This kind of schedule results in a pressure-cooker existence when everything goes as planned. But how about emergencies? When the weather is bad and the preschool center is closed, who takes the day off from work? Which parent? Supposing the center calls to say that their child is sick and needs to be taken home or to the doctor? Supposing one of the parents has a meeting that lasts beyond the close of the work day? There used to be a kind neighbor who could be called on in an emergency to pick up the daughter from the center. But now she has just taken a job herself and she needs a kind neighbor or relative to help *her*. What happens when one of the parents has to travel and is barely accessible by phone for two weeks abroad?

The kind of lifestyle I have described poses problems at work. Let me outline these in a series of questions. How can a superstar, one who is seen as an energetic, high-achieving, dedicated individual willing to give the company unlimited time, shift gears after becoming a parent without damaging his or her professional image? How can a person demonstrate seriousness and commitment and still leave the office on time? Can a person be seen as a committed professional and avoid late meetings and evening dinners? The kind of person I have described is, unfortunately, not seen as a really dedicated manager.

The business environment is still, by and large, unyielding and unsympathetic to working parents' schedules. But working parents now represent a dominant lifestyle in our society. Corporations could initiate policies that would ease working parents' problems. One of them is flextime, but this must be accompanied by a change in the prevalent attitude that working late or overtime is a measure of seriousness, commitment, and professional interest. Flexplace, allowing work to be performed partly at home and partly in the office, would also ease the strain. There are many management tasks that could, in fact, be completed more efficiently at home, away from constant interruptions. A third policy that would help is cafeteria-style benefits. If parents were free to pick and choose among various benefits, this would do away with needless duplications, such as both having medical insurance. The cost of the foregone benefit could be applied to others which could help working parents more, such as additional vacation time, leave for care of sick children, and the like.

If employers took advantage of the new tax laws to subsidize child care costs, many a parent would opt for that benefit rather than for retirement benefits. Options for part-time employment at the managerial level need to be explored. It is still the case that most companies have no provision for other than full-time work in management. It seems to me that many parents might choose a 4-, 5-, or 6-hour day or a 3- or 4-day week. While this might slow the pace of their professional advancement, it should not stall it altogether. It would surely improve the quality of their complicated and demanding lives. In Sweden, legislation guarantees parents of young children the right to part-time employment with proportional fringe benefits if they desire it.

The most important change we could make in the United States would be a change in the attitude toward parenting. Being a parent is a normal stage in the life cycle of an adult. When business recognizes this, as it recognizes that being young is normal and being old is normal, then the quality of life of working parents will improve.

One Family's Decision: A Leave of Absence

Margaret Coffey

How did I come to decide to take a leave of absence from my job as a marketing manager? The story starts five years ago. At that time, we were living in Boston. The day I registered at a well-known Eastern business school, I found out that I was pregnant. So I had my first major management decision to make. I decided to try to stick it out, but I lasted only six weeks because I was sick in those early months.

The next fall, I thought long and hard about whether or not to start again. By then, our baby was three or four months old. I had deferred admission twice by then and I figured it was this year or never. Another factor was that my husband and I had started a family business with a number of employees. Life insurance agents kept coming around; I could not help but think we needed a lot of insur-

Margaret Coffey joined Corning Glass Works as marketing manager of Corning Biosystems in 1979 and has been on leave from that post since 1982. A 1972 graduate of Mount Holyoke College in biology and art, Coffey received her M.B.A. from Harvard Graduate School of Business Administration in 1979. Her work experience includes serving as business manager and director of Coffey Corporation, a rowing shell manufacturer; as computer sales representative of Digital Equipment Corporation; as first woman computer sales representative at Honeywell Information Systems; as a biology researcher for Woods Hole Oceanographic Institute; and as an editor for Radio Free Europe in Munich.

ance. Suppose something happened to my husband. So I decided to go to business school for my own life insurance purposes.

The first day at school one of the professors asked, "What are you coming to school for when you have a baby?" I was one of eighty-eight students in the section. Only eight were women; I was the only one who had a baby. The professor said I was crazy. That was a message I heard often during the time I was earning the M.B.A.: "Why are you here? We can't really believe you are serious."

When I finished, I wanted to go back and work in our family business. But the salary offers I got turned my husband's head, I think. He said, "Why don't you take one of those?" And he would add, "If you don't, you're crazy." So, when a corporation in a small town offered me a post as marketing manager, I took it seriously. A person does not want to be thought of as crazy. But the company did not have many women in management and there were no child care facilities in town for our two-and-a-half-year-old daughter. Six months later, I learned that the company's foundation was opening a child care center. The management had recognized that if they were serious about attracting women, they would have to. So I joined the company, enrolled our daughter in that fine center, and all went well until I went to Europe for a month. When I came home, I was so glad to see my husband that, next thing I knew, I was pregnant again. I did not foresee that this would be a problem, although I should assure you that juggling one baby and a job is not as easy as it may sound, even when there is a good child care center. It is very demanding psychologically and physically.

When the second baby was born, I thought, "I love it all. I don't want to give up anything." I planned to go back to work in six weeks. Well, that stretched into six months. I went back; three weeks later, I got a bad backache, which the doctor said was stress related. Three weeks after that, I had palpitations of the heart, also related to stress.

Stress? It seemed to me that I had everything under control. But then I had to accept it. Other people were telling me, for the third time in my life, that I was crazy and I was beginning to think they were right. On the job, I was beginning to see that if I kept working as hard as I was, I could be promoted and move right up the corporate ladder. That had been one of my goals. I figured that the higher you go and the more money you earn, the more personal freedom you have.

But I was wrong. The more they pay you, the more they own you, in a way. I felt my personal freedom diminishing instead of enlarging. I felt guilty because I could not spend more time both with the company and with my children. The issue of personal freedom became more and more important. I thought, "If I work really hard, maybe, in five years, I'll be a vice president." That means $100,000. But it also means that if you are home on a Saturday enjoying yourself and the chairman of the board phones up and says, "Go to France," you go to France. At this point in my life, I don't want that kind of impingement on my personal freedom. I want to be able to see my children, to go home when I want to, and so on. I felt under increasing pressure to make a decision.

There were three things pulling on my life this last winter—my job, my two children and my husband, and the family business and its ten to fifteen employees. What could be changed? I certainly didn't want to give up the family, and I couldn't convince my husband to give up his business. The only thing I could change in the equation was the job. So I went to management and told them I was resigning. They have me down officially as on "leave of absence" in case, as some say, I "come to my senses."

Now I work half time, twenty hours a week, for my husband, running the small business. I have the option of going back to work for the company part time or a few days a week or as a consultant, when I want to. They might well not have given me that option if I had not said I was resigning. I guess the message is that unless you push for your options as a woman with a family, you are not likely to get any.

When you come out of an M.B.A. program and start juggling a career and a family, you are going to increase the physical and psychological stress on your body. You ought to recognize that, set your own personal priorities, and try to stick by them. We all want to be happy and live a long life. When we start making decisions that compromise this, it can lead to disillusionment and dissatisfaction in later life.

As a final note, you may be interested to hear that my company is realizing that women are a most valuable asset. This summer, they plan to initiate a new policy that will give full-time benefits to part-time people. Some men there are saying, "This is a great deal for the corporation. Women really are a cheap resource that we ought to be tapping into." No matter what the motive, it constitutes a real opportunity for women who are doing what I did: making hard decisions based on personal priorities.

Personal Choices

Deborah K. Smith

Managing a career and a family is clearly a matter of setting priorities and making choices. I would like to talk about some of the personal choices I have made in working to achieve a balance in life. First, let me give you some background about myself, starting with my job. I am a manager of human resources. I have responsibility for management development, training, employee communications, organization development consulting, personnel systems and reporting, and personnel research, which includes the supervision of psychologists who do test validation, special studies, and attitude surveys. It is a very challenging position in both scope and responsibility.

Deborah K. Smith is manager of human resources in the Business Systems Group, Xerox Corporation, a post she has held since January 1980. Smith earned the B.A. with highest distinction in history from the University of Rochester in 1968, where she was elected to Phi Beta Kappa. She was awarded the M.A. at Cornell University in 1971, where she completed all requirements for the Ph.D. except for the dissertation. At Xerox, Smith has been employment representative, senior training specialist, and personnel program manager of the Business Systems Group and manager of personnel operations, of personnel and education, and of personnel administrative services of the General Services Division.

You should also know that I have two boys, one who is seven and the other, four and a half. I went through both pregnancies while I was managing at the corporation and took six weeks off for each. The first worked out well. The six weeks went right into the Christmas holidays; I had enough time to get rested and was eager to get back. The second was different. I was nine months pregnant when I moved into a new line management position. I had no technical expertise in data processing, and the group was facing a critical audit for which they were not prepared. I spent the ninth month with them, went into the hospital, and kept in touch by phone from there. In the next weeks, we had meetings in my home and I went into the office part time. I never really stopped working. This was a matter of personal choice.

In addition to the job and my family, I am also involved in the community. I am on three boards of directors, I teach a business seminar at a local women's college, and I am on three judicial commissions appointed by the governor. It is hard to see how life could be more full. When I talk about trying to balance all of this, I am talking not only about myself but about several other women I know who are doing the same kinds of things. How is it possible, we ask ourselves, to have a family, a responsible job, a serious commitment to community work, and to maintain your balance? The answer is to understand your priorities and to make deliberate decisions when there is a conflict between them.

First, about the job. It has been my experience that the higher up you go in terms of responsibility, the more flexibility you get to exercise. While there are more demands requiring more of your time, you also have more control over how you spend your time. For example, if you have an emergency or want to attend a function at school, it is usually possible to change meetings, or go to the office a little later, or make different child care arrangements. Because the meetings may be meetings you called and the people attending may report to you, you may have the ability to change your schedule. In general, I have found that you need to be well organized and flexible. And you need to make difficult choices when demands are in conflict.

For child care, I have a person who comes to the house in the morning, stays with the boys all day, and then goes home. She has a car and gets them every place they need to go. As the boys have grown older, she has become more and more of a chauffeur, taking them to story hour at the library, to swimming lessons, to their friends' houses, to nursery school. Between the time she drops them off and picks them up, she does light cleaning, picks up groceries, and so on. That kind of arrangement gives me lots of flexibility. If both my husband and I have an early meeting, she can be there early. If we both need to come home late, she can stay late.

This is expensive but, in child care as in other things, you get what you pay for. I have also found that the better you treat people, the better they will treat you and your children, and the more a part of your family they become. To be sure, there are problems. Sometimes the children are sick; sometimes there is a meeting that cannot be missed. I have found that I have been able to work around these things but only by understanding *my* priorities and making choices between them.

An important thing to remember is that husbands cannot be neglected. A spouse needs attention, just as you do. Many people forget this—both in relationships where both partners work and in those where only one does. They forget to pay attention to one another.

You also need to have time for yourself. This is what most of us trade off when we start working in a responsible job: our own time for exercise class, for reading novels, for hobbies, and for sleep. If you add up all the responsibilities and all the time they take, it is clear that something has to give. In my case, time for myself is what I have given up.

A key to keeping it all together is organization. When you are trying to do lots of things at once, you have to be organized. I make lists. That may sound like a small thing, but I have found if I do plan things ahead and get them out of the way, then I have the time to do the things I really want to do with my family. I also try to make fun out of things other people may regard as chores. Planning ahead, time management—it really comes down to *you* controlling events, not letting them control you, and not letting other people make decisions on how you spend your time.

In our concern for our husbands, our children, and all the other people in our lives, we sometimes forget about ourselves. We can't do that. We must find time for ourselves and our own friends, time with other women who are trying to deal with the same issues. We have to keep reminding ourselves what we want out of life, what is really important to us. That's critical. What's right for me may not work for you. There is more than one way to look at things. So I urge you to look at what you really want and make your choices and live with them. It is not easy but it surely is worthwhile.

Discussion

The presentations of the panelists elicited a wide range of questions and comments. Part of the focus was on image. Was it true, some students asked, that one had to wear a uniform in a corporate setting? Consensus among several panelists was that one did have to look the part. One remarked that nobody dictated what she wore at home. She felt it wasn't too much of a concession to wear conventional clothes in the work setting. "If you don't," she warned, "you have to spend too much time persuading people that there are brains under those beads in your hair."

One questioner said she felt faintly demoralized when she heard about women who were able to hold all the balls up in the air, who were able to do everything—job, family, community work—all at once. She urged those present to not look down on those who are not superwomen. "Let's give one another support and friendships and teach one another things," she said, "rather than leaving some of us with the impression that we are of a lesser species."

How are minority women faring? The consensus was that, in the companies represented, minority women are fairly well represented at the middle management level. But they, like white women, are not yet in top management.

Alice Cook, professor emerita of industrial and labor relations at Cornell University, noted that she had undertaken studies of working mothers in nine countries and that much of what she had heard at this conference confirmed her findings.[1] All over the world, she said, working mothers organize their lives so tightly and effectively that it is clear that they have considerable organizational and managerial talent. Cook's question was, "To what extent is this talent recognized? Are these women eligible for higher level management based on the skills they demonstrate as working mothers?"

Eleanor Byrnes agreed that the talents for organizing family life and work life are related; both are "results oriented." On the job, women are able to see what needs to be done, to organize the project,

---

1. Alice H. Cook, *The Working Mother: A Survey of Problems and Programs in Nine Countries* (Ithaca: New York State School of Industrial and Labor Relations, 1978).

and to complete it. If you can do a task more competently than the next person, you are clearly going to be in line for promotion. This is not to say that the details of your family situation are known to all. They are not, as a rule. How you want to organize your life, how fast you aim to move up a career ladder, how tightly organized you feel your life must be—these are decisions, Byrnes said, that only you can make. "You should think about them long and hard," she advised. It may be, she remarked, that you may not be ready to rush ahead to that next step on the career ladder right now. You may not feel ready to make that commitment of energy right now. Each of us has only so much energy. We should expend it on what we choose to do.

Another listener remarked that what she heard from the speakers suggested to her that women should be resigned to the fact that they have to take responsibility for the child care, the home care, meal preparation, and so on—either doing it or making arrangements for others to do it. Patricia Oesterle opined that it depends on the marriage. It also depends on where each of you is in your career. "My husband is at a point where he needs to travel a great deal. I have more time right now, so the child care is my responsibility, mainly." Another panelist said she felt that while some things have changed, child care is still, for the majority of couples, the responsibility of the wife. She allowed that this might change in the future but reiterated that it has not changed yet.

"My husband is quite liberated—intellectually," a participant said. "He helps with everything. But I still feel as though it is all my responsibility because I am managing the tasks. In fact, this is one of the responsibilities I put on myself: the role of manager at home. There you are." Another participant said she wanted to emphasize that we all have choice in that respect. It is nowhere written that we women have to manage at home. We just do.

"My husband passed up an opportunity for a promotion because he wants more time with the children," another listener said. Eleanor Byrnes reported that no men in her bank had requested paternity leave yet; Margaret Coffey said that in her former company, the mother has six weeks' leave for maternity. Then six months additional leave is offered, which either parent can take. The same benefits are offered to adoptive parents, Coffey said. Not as many men as women have taken advantage of it, but some men have, Coffey said.

To what extent have secretarial people been able to work from home? Only one panelist was able to report on that. She said there had been one experimental project that had gotten a great deal of media coverage. But the fact is, she said, this is very expensive and the benefits do not seem to outweigh the heavy costs. Another participant remarked that the introduction of home terminals did not seem to automatically promise benefits. "That just makes it possible for women to be expected to do two jobs at once, alone at home. Terrific."

Another listener said she had been thinking about the problem of asking for special things, as a working mother. Managers should perhaps not have to ask or even explain why they need to leave early some afternoon, she reasoned. But so long as we think we have to explain our every move, we may be held back.

Panelist Margaret Coffey held that only time can change certain stereotypes. When she was in college in the late 1960s, she thought that the old role stereotypes were gone, that marriages were all equal, and that people really were free to be what they were best suited to being. Now her daughter comes home and says, "Doctors are men and nurses are women." Same old thing. By the same token, many couples have tried a strict division of labor at home. "I'll be in charge of the downstairs and you do the upstairs." We tried that, Coffey reported. But then you can't even walk in our upstairs. Now I say to myself, "Maybe this will change in my granddaughter's generation."

One listener said she felt we are living in a time of transition. A panelist agreed. Her mother and her husband's mother did things a certain way and she had been brought up to believe that that was the only way. "Clean the house from top to bottom once a week, wash and iron the sheets and pillowcases once a week, bake cookies once a week." It is hard to change these patterns. For some of us, brought up that way, and married to men brought up with those expectations, it is almost too late to change.

The suggestion was made that you can buy those services and go out to eat as much as you can. "If we get home late and have grilled cheese sandwiches and soup for dinner, nobody can complain." Compromises have to be made. There is no right and wrong in this area. It comes down to what both people can live with. The worst compromise is the one that results in guilt or anger or discord.

Another panelist remarked that for dual career couples one major hassle seems to be who will do the dishes. One solution is to use paper plates; another is to eat out a lot. Another symptom of the transitional era we are living in is the fact that, when people come to my house, I have to remind myself to not apologize for the way things look. If it is a mess, I have to bite my tongue, she said, to keep from saying, "He made a mess; the children made a mess." But at the very least, I won't apologize for it.

An older woman said she understood that perfectly. But, she said, things really are changing. She had worked as a manager for many years, she said; her sons had taken it for granted that she would and that their wives would. She said with some pride that her sons were making equal partnerships with their wives and that they had learned that attitude where all children should learn it: at home.

CHAPTER 5

Recommended Readings

Jennie Farley

On the subject of women in management, there is no lack of reading matter, ranging from serious academic studies to foolish ones and from provocative advice books to dreary articles listing virtues good managers are said to practice. Popular writers and, less often, academic researchers both sometimes err in assuming that women managers are now men's equals. In fact, although women managers are rising higher than ever before, that is still not very high and certainly not often into top management. Only 8 percent of all women workers are classified as managers while 15 percent of men workers are.[1] The male/female pay gap still yawns wide: for every dollar a

Jennie Farley, associate professor of industrial and labor relations at Cornell University, holds three degrees from Cornell: the B.A. in English (1954), the M.S. (1969), and the Ph.D. (1970), both of the latter in development sociology. She served as cofounder and first director of the university's Women's Studies Program. Farley edited *Sex Discrimination in Higher Education: Strategies for Equality* (ILR Publications, 1981) and is author of *Affirmative Action and the Woman Worker: Guidelines for Personnel Management* (American Management Associations, 1979) and *Academic Women and Employment Discrimination: A Critical Annotated Bibliography* (ILR Publications, 1982).

1. U.S. Department of Labor, Bureau of Labor Statistics, *Employment and Earnings*, October 1982, Table A-22, "Employed Persons by Occupation, Race, and Sex," p. 24.

man manager earns for year-round full-time work, a woman manager earns sixty-one cents.[2] Some twenty-five hundred top corporate managers earn $100,000 or more per year; of these, a scant fifteen are women.[3] One reason is that women and men do different work. Women manage departments in retail stores, small eating establishments, and, most often, offices; men manage businesses, industrial organizations, unions, and virtually everything else. The sharp increase in the last thirty years in the number of women working for pay has not been matched by a proportionate increase in the number of women managers.[4] Why have women remained in the ranks of the managed and the followers while men manage and lead? What should women be doing to move up faster? Academic researchers have sought to answer the first question; many popular writers, the second.

As Judith Leavitt discovered when she prepared her useful bibliography on women in management, no fewer than five hundred pertinent journal articles, reports, books, newspaper articles, and dissertations appeared in the 1970s. Reviewing the research literature through 1979, Linda Keller Brown found it to represent a wide range of disciplinary perspectives but to be of uneven quality. In 1980, Carol Greenwald reviewed and summarized recent research, finding investigators dissatisfied with the state of the art, calling for different methodology and more comprehensive analyses.

Some of the work was clearly outside the mainstream. Anthropologist Lionel Tiger (*Men in Groups*, 1969) traced women's lack of success in management to their lack of an "instinct for bonding," a characteristic which men, he said, had. Graham Staines and his colleagues identified what they called the "Queen Bee syndrome" (*Psychology Today*, 1974), that is, successful women's purported unwillingness to reach back to help junior women. Colette Dowling identified the "major force" holding women back from

2. Nancy F. Rytina, "Earnings of Men and Women: A Look at Specific Occupations," *Monthly Labor Review* 105, no. 4 (April 1982): 25–31.

3. Anne Field, "The Powers That Be," *Ms.*, December 1982, p. 78.

4. Linda Keller Brown, *The Woman Manager in the United States: A Research Analysis and Bibliography* (Washington, D.C.: Business and Professional Women's Foundation, 1981).

achievement as their wish to be taken care of (*The Cinderella Complex: Women's Hidden Fear of Independence*, 1981). These theories received little serious attention. More sophisticated theories have received serious attention—and have deserved to—because there is evidence to support them. Psychologist Matina Horner found that some competent young women fear success because they believe it will cost them socially. Young women usually enter college with less preparation in mathematics than their male counterparts have. This avoidance of mathematics proves crippling for women, as for the men who manifest it, because it narrows so drastically the range of college majors and future careers they can pursue. The hypothesis that sex difference in mathematical reasoning ability may be traced to biological influences was heralded in an article in the November 1982 *Reader's Digest*, reprinted from *Playboy*.

Research results are sometimes misinterpreted ("all women fear success"; "all women avoid math"). When this happens, some women are made anxious. An apparent difference between the sexes in brain functioning reported responsibly in the September issue of *Science '82* caused a feminist reader to wonder why research on sex differences is being done at all "and lately, so fervently. Are we working toward a master plan of dictating to women and men what they should do and how, based on unassailable 'scientific' evidence?"[5] Anthropologist Donald Symons (*The Evolution of Human Sexuality*, 1979) has been accused of attempting to buttress "the dominant male theory—a kind of scientific absolution for promiscuity, philandering, prostitution, and pornography." ("Symons Says," by Roger Bingham, January/February, *Science '83*.) Psychologist Naomi Weisstein, reviewing theories of sociobiology (*Ms.*, November 1982), concluded, "Biology has always been used as a curse against women. From Darwin to Desmond Morris, from Freud to Robin Fox . . . the message has rarely changed: men are biologically suited to their life of power, pleasure, and privilege, and women must accept subordination, sacrifice, and submission."

Many of the "how to" books have been as controversial.

---

5. Janne Gutreimer, Letter to the Editor, "Advice and Dissent," *Science '82* 3 no. 9 (November 1982): 16, 20.

Women readers have been urged to learn power games, to take risks, to dress for success, to be more assertive in language and behavior, to manage time better, to set long-range career plans instead of waiting to see what develops, and to otherwise remedy what are said to be feminine deficits. The books based on these single factor theories, while limited, are not dull. If they tend to make outrageous generalizations, they at least acknowledge that there could be such a thing as an ambitious woman.

In the 1960s, a book called *The Managerial Mind* managed to include only two references to women: one example from a personnel text of an unruly woman subordinate about whose case the male union steward and the male manager argued and one to the way in which managers "differ from men and women in other vocations." A 1971 guide to *Routes to the Executive Suite* included not one reference to women, signifying perhaps that, in the author's view, no feminine foot had trod any of those routes nor was likely to. The next year, *Personal and Professional Success for Women* was published; it noted that there are young women who "fit nicely the clerical worker/errand girl role" and asserted that "the majority of women prefer that role and the majority of just-graduated young women seek only marriage."

By 1977, there was allusion (at last) to the balancing act that women who are both serious about their careers and committed to their children must try to sustain. The author of *The New Executive Woman* considered the problem and concluded that the optimum solution was not to have children. But, she noted, one advantage of having a large family of five children would be that the mother would then be less threatening to her male colleagues because she would be seen as feminine and motherly.

In 1978 came *The Effective Woman Manager,* whose author promised in the introduction that it would not be a "Betty Friedan tract or Margaret Mead treatise" nor "another conventional textbook on the principles of management." But with its tedious quizzes, bromidic guidelines ("Be neither dominant nor dominated"), and lists of virtues to practice, the book was in no danger of having more influence than writings by social critic Friedan or distinguished anthropologist Mead.

In 1981, *Changing Times* reported that dynamic career women were choosing to give up their jobs to stay home with their children: "Meet the liberated mother . . . battling the notion that a woman's worth should be measured by the size of her paycheck." "One key to succeeding as a full-time mother," the anonymous author advised, "is to choose your role freely and have confidence in your decision" ("Making the Switch from Job to Full-time Mother," *Changing Times,* April 1981). And in November 1982, women managers were urged to choose love over success, thus making the "selfless choice." Natalie Gittelson, writing in *McCall's* ("Success and Love: Do I Have to Choose?") advised women to realize that the "workplace was never meant to provide the kind of nurturant values, such as caring, fulfillment and personal growth" which can only be found "in the realm of love, home and family."

The most popular "how to" books in the late seventies and early eighties took a different tack. They advised women managers to get the very most out of their jobs that they could and to fight for promotion to higher-paying posts. Top jobs are few and far between but they are so much fun to do that getting them and keeping them is worth the struggle. How to move up? Work hard, the writers said; get the right training; keep your eye out for opportunities and grab them when they come; be on time for meetings; spell people's names right; don't sleep where you work; treat the people of both sexes in your work circle and outside it like human beings; and, above all else, keep the hand, whether manicured or not, out of the cooky jar. This sensible counsel was often illustrated by examples which, while not exactly based on research, did catch the attention. A quiz in *Management Strategies for Women* (Thompson and Wood, 1980) offered problems of this ilk: "Your husband is uncomfortable with your working overtime since your staff, also working overtime, is all male." The woman manager is invited to select among the following solutions:

1. To avoid guilt feelings, don't work overtime if your husband disapproves.

2. Help your husband recognize the true and legitimate demands of your job, which include occasional overtime hours and travel.

3. Divorce your husband. Good jobs are more difficult to find than good husbands.

4. Cut off your husband's allowance until he shapes up.

While the new writing eschews rehashes of Theory X (results-oriented) and Theory Y (people-oriented) management philosophies, it does sometimes give advice which is contradictory. Jo Foxworth (*Wising Up*) says that if a woman manager cannot keep her supervisor from sexually harassing her, she should quit. Another advisor (*Jane Trahey on Women and Power*) favors complaining to management in a group. Foxworth says class action lawsuits do not help women, even if they could be won, which, she says, they cannot: "Fighting a corporation that vast in a case with so many far-flung ramifications is like fighting the telephone company." Other writers may be surprised at that advice, since they cite successful suits as bringing about welcome change at Chase Manhattan Bank (Larwood and Wood, *Women in Management*), the Bank of America (Gordon and Strober, *Bringing Women into Management*), the New York Times (O'Reilly, *The Girl I Left Behind*), Western Electric (Bird, *Everything a Woman Needs to Know . . .*), and, to be sure, at America's largest private employer of women, AT&T (Hennig and Jardim, *The Managerial Woman*).

If academic studies tend to be too specific, management advice books tend to be too general. Blanchard and Johnson (*The One-Minute Manager*) suggest that sixty-second "praisings" and "reprimands" can take care of human relationships in the workplace for weeks. And Silcox (*Woman Time: Personal Time Management for Women Only*) notes that women can save time in managing their sex lives by avoiding commitment to one person.

The best writing on why women are where they are in management and how individuals and organizations can change that situation avoids such excesses. The most thoughtful analyses are still Kreps's *Women and the American Economy*, Kanter's *Men and Women of the Corporation*, and Harragan's *Games Mother Never Taught You*. Forty-six other readings are recommended here, chosen because they represent good scholarship based on evidence or good sense based on experience and because they are interesting.

Some authors speculate about the future. It is almost as exhilarating to consider the possibilities as it must be to be among the first to go through the formerly closed door to the executive suite. If the authors of the advice books are to be believed, life for women at the top has an extra delicious and richly deserved satisfaction because they beat the odds. As television executive Joan Ganz Cooney put it, she's been bossed and she's been a boss and being a boss is better.[6]

---

6. Lindsy Van Gelder, "Okay, You're in Power; Now What Do You Do: Interviews," *Ms.*, December 1982, p. 45.

Bibliography

Adams, Jane. *Women on Top: Success Patterns and Personal Growth.* New York: Berkley, 1981.

The author lets the sixty women she interviewed speak for themselves in long, astonishingly candid reports which touch on their sex lives, their children, their tragedies at work, and their triumphs there. Adams groups her respondents into "fast track women," "principled strivers," "corporate women," "entrepreneurs," "inheritors," "public successes," and "mentored successes." She weaves in reports of research studies and identifies support for theories in her own findings. Sample observations on stress: even though there is pressure at work, the real tension for some women comes from personal life struggles; the greatest increase in stress among women workers is not among those in management but among those in routinized, low-paying jobs. She quotes one of her successes as remarking, "My first association with women who were my professional peers was a great source of relief to me. It was like taking off your girdle for the first time in nearly fifteen years. My migraine headaches disappeared and so did the skin rashes I'd had since I was twenty-five—since my first promotion, as a matter of fact."

Bartholet, Elizabeth. "Application of Title VII to Jobs in High Places." *Harvard Law Review* 95, no. 5 (March 1982): 947–1027.

The law, specifically Title VII of the Civil Rights Act of 1964, has been effective in protecting those in blue-collar jobs from discrimination, this author argues. But, she says, the courts have been far less likely to subject employment policies affecting managers and professionals to "the brilliant light of Title VII inquiry." When grievants have challenged methods of choosing or promoting managers, judges have left those methods "largely in the shadows, unexamined and undisturbed." This judicial deference is what makes it imperative for plaintiffs to fashion class action suits, she notes. She provides many interesting examples of sex discrimination suits brought by women professionals and concludes, based on evidence carefully reviewed, that imaginative alternatives to traditional selection methods should be considered, "alternatives that we should consider if our only concern is quality, but that we have failed to consider because of the tendency of those who are 'in' to perpetuate the systems that got them there."

Basil, Douglas C., with Edna Traver. *Women in Management.* New York: Dunellen, 1972.

This book is the report of a study supported by the Business and Professional

Women's Foundation which sought to determine why there were so few women managers in 1965. Three hundred sixteen executives (of whom 102 were women) responded to a mailed questionnaire. Results showed that managers believed that women had inadequate experience and lacked three other pertinent characteristics: geographic mobility, appropriate education and training, and the necessary drive and motivation.

Bird, Caroline. *The Two-Paycheck Marriage.* New York: Pocketbooks, 1980.

A full and careful study of five thousand responses to a survey published in *Family Circle* magazine in 1976. A brisk and straightforward writer, Bird sets out to study the effect of work on various aspects of family life and succeeds in summarizing her own study and many others well. One of her more provocative conclusions is that, if women move into top management posts, this may relieve men from having to prove, over and over, that they are not women.

Bird, Caroline, with Marjorie Godfrey and Helen Mandelbaum. *Everything a Woman Needs to Know to Get Paid What She's Worth . . . in the 1980's.* New York: Bantam, 1981.

Reading this book is like having a talk with a knowledgeable but busy acquaintance. Completely focused on work (as opposed to family) issues, the information is organized as paragraph-long answers to questions ("What work can a woman do to earn more money?" "Go where the men are. . . ." "Should I join a union?" "By all means. . . ."). Bird is guarded about the utility of management training courses, less committed than many other writers to the option of going back to school, less sanguine about the utility of filing a lawsuit. Her sixteen-page resource section, a model of careful organization, contains up-to-date information on books, courses, organizations, and legal rights.

Brown, Linda Keller. "Review Essay: Women and Business Management." *Signs* 5, no. 2 (Winter 1979): 266–88.

The definitive review of the academic literature. Brown concludes that one weakness of the approach to date is that it has failed to take into account that the few women who have made it into top management arrived there by very different routes than those to be followed by young women with M.B.A. degrees in the early eighties and that these two paths both differ in turn from the generation in between.

Corporations and Two-Career Families: Directions for the Future. A Report Based on the Findings of Two National Surveys. Washington, D.C.: Catalyst Career and Family Center, 1981.

This nonprofit organization surveyed 374 of the Fortune 1300 corporations and 815 two-career couples to determine what employers can do in terms of child care, flexible benefits, nepotism rules, and relocation problems. One telling finding: corporate perceptions about who cares for children have changed, with 83 percent of those responding saying they believed that men were increasingly feeling the need to share parenting responsibilities. However, Baila Zeitz, director of this study, reported that "the change in attitudes about parenting has not yet been reflected in corporate policy." Catalyst is a good source of other research reports that provide helpful ammunition for those interested in initiating or speeding corporate change.

Fader, Shirley Sloan. *Successfully Ever After: A Young Woman's Guide to Career Happiness.* New York: McGraw-Hill, 1982.

This manual will be of particular interest to women who have not been to college and are working up from first-line supervisory jobs. Among the practical chapters are several on benefits, legal rights, evaluating your company's commitment to equal employment opportunity, and outwitting job testers. This controversial chapter is divided into sections: drawings, sentence completion, stories about picture cards, inkblot tests, in-basket exercises, and other assessment tests. Whether you see giving away this information as perfidy or sisterhood may well depend on whether you give such tests or take them.

Families at Work: Strengths and Strains. The General Mills American Family Report, 1980–81. Minneapolis: General Mills, 1981.

This is the report of a survey conducted for General Mills by Louis Harris and Associates of six different groups: a national cross section of 1,503 adults in families, 235 teenagers, 104 human resource executives from Fortune 1300 companies, 56 labor leaders, 49 leaders in the "pro-family" movement, and 52 feminist leaders. They uncovered many conflicts in attitudes toward proposed solutions to the problems associated with the tension between full-time work and family responsibilities.

Farley, Jennie. *Affirmative Action and the Woman Worker: Guidelines for Personnel Management.* New York: AMACOM, 1979.

One person's opinion about what affirmative action should mean in recruitment, selection, and training of women. Includes sections on day-to-day problems from styling women's names to office romances.

Forisha, Barbara L., and Goldman, Barbara H. *Outsiders on the Inside: Women and Organizations.* Englewood Cliffs, N.J.: Prentice-Hall, 1981.

A collection of papers that serves as an excellent introduction to the study of sex roles in society. For women managers, the most pertinent is the only chapter by a nonacademic, management consultant Patricia Kosinar. "Socialization and Self Esteem: Women in Management" is a crisp rundown of what the author believes we have learned femininity means and what aspects of masculinity we are trying to integrate into our self images. Kosinar believes that some women are haunted by the fear that being successful is making them less feminine, as they define it. This, she says, results in many secret sadnesses.

Foxworth, Jo. *Boss Lady: An Executive Woman Talks about Making It.* New York: Thomas Y. Crowell, 1978.

Mainly autobiographical, this book begins in a narrative vein: "I was born and reared in Mississippi, where the choice was between early liberation and more or less permanent pregnancy." How did she make it to the presidency of her own advertising agency? She was a disaster at sports when young (the only undergraduate woman to fail a physical education course called "Rest in the Room"; she didn't rest at prescribed times, apparently); she was fat, so felt she had to be smart-alecky. She tosses off a theory that female achievers were often overweight adolescents. The best practical advice is in chapter 13 ("The Inquisition"), which gives sound counsel on fending off queries about one's personal life or marital status, and some observations about giving a talk. Every now and then, Foxworth says chapters in a sentence. For example, "Keep mousey quiet" about it if you are cohabiting; all may seem liberal on the surface in your office; they aren't.

Foxworth, Jo. *Wising Up: The Mistakes Women Make in Business and How to Avoid Them.* New York: Dell, 1981.

The tone of this funny book is set by the author's opening observation that most companies operate in a state of continuing confusion. It will be most useful to women who, like the author, work in a glamor industry. Participative management? She dismisses that with a few paragraphs in chapter 6. Possibly the most instructive is chapter 7, which recounts problems otherwise confident women encounter when they try to ask for a raise.

Goffman, Erving. *Gender Advertisements.* New York: Harper Colophon Books, 1979.

This is a brilliant analysis of male and female images in advertising. Vivian Gornick has contributed an insightful and respectful introduction; Goffman's text is illustrated by five hundred pictures of advertisements. "Commercial photographs, of course, involve carefully performed poses presented in the style of being 'only natural.' But it is argued that actual gender expressions are artful poses, too." Sociologist Goffman has gently shown us how some of us grew up thinking how we wanted to be. In all these photographs, nary a woman manager.

Gordon, Francine E., and Strober, Myra H. *Bringing Women into Management.* New York: McGraw-Hill, 1975.

This is a book by experts, as useful for women who aspire to management as for women and men who are already there and committed to bringing more women in. The authors summarize the major problems as four: misconceptions about women's capabilities as managers; inhospitable informal structures; recruitment, hiring, and promotion policies; and perceived incompatibilities between career and family goals. They offer sound suggestions (including case studies) for resolving the first three and note that the fourth problem "may prove the most challenging to individuals and organizations." The book includes definitive chapters by sociologist Cynthia Fuchs Epstein, psychologists Carol Nagy Jacklin and Eleanor Emmons Maccoby, economist Myra Strober, and organizational specialist Francine Gordon.

Gordon, Suzanne. "Dressed for Success: The New Corporate Feminism." *Nation* 236, no. 5 (February 5, 1983): 1; 143; 146–47.

Women have been sold a bill of goods, this author argues. Business has redefined and depoliticized "one of the most compelling social movements of the late twentieth century" into "corporate feminism—a brand of feminism designed to sell books and magazines, three-piece suits, airline tickets, Scotch, cigarettes and, most important, corporate America's message, which runs: Yes, women were discriminated against in the past, but that unfortunate mistake has been remedied; now every woman can attain wealth, prestige and power by dint of individual rather than collective effort." Women are being advised that sticking with other women is now inappropriate; each must look out for number one; each must dress for success. But, this author holds, "Standardization in fashion is indicative of a more extensive standardization" and "Women cannot do it differently because they're not allowed to." The article includes chilling quotations from management advice books and articles for women.

Greenwald, Carol S. *Women in Management.* Scarsdale, N.Y.: Work in America Institute, 1980.

This overview of the literature traces two lines of explanation for women's lack of progress in management: either women are by nature less qualified or men are discriminating against them. Includes a careful and accurate annotated bibliography.

Hall, Francine S., and Hall, Douglas T. *The Two-Career Couple.* Reading, Mass.: Addison-Wesley, 1979.

This book of advice is based in part on research and in part on the authors' own experience in trying to have both serious careers and deep commitment to their children and to each other. Beginning with the assertion that most two-career families are not living a glamorous life, but a frantic one, the Halls provide numerous examples of problems and solutions to them. The most instructive sections are "Making the House Work," "Loving versus Working," and "Splitting Up or Staying Together." Two interesting quizzes are the "Romanticism Scale" (to ascertain how romantic you are compared to others) and the "Holmes Stress Scale" (to predict the likelihood of getting physically or emotionally ill based on the number of life changes you have experienced recently). The authors observe that the return of wives to the work force does not necessarily increase the number of work-related affairs (nobody has time), that over-involvement in work on the part of either or both partners can strain a relationship (whether or not both have paying jobs), and that finding two satisfying jobs in the same place is the first big hurdle the two-career couple must overcome, but it is not the last. The tone is not preachy; the authors readily acknowledge that there are no hard and fast rules of conduct in two-career marriages, only different approaches to trying to make it all work the way the partners want it to for themselves, their children, and their careers.

Harlan, Anne, and Weiss, Carol. "Final Report from *Moving Up: Women in Managerial Careers.*" Working Paper No. 86. Wellesley, Mass.: Wellesley College Center for Research on Women, 1981.

Describing their study of one hundred female and male managers at two large concerns, these authors said they uncovered two subtle forms of sex discrimination they had not expected. Middle management supervisors preferred older, less aggressive women, while senior managers wanted young, aggressive dynamos. "The women who might have fit that mold weren't being promoted." A second problem emerged in the area of supervisory feedback and correction. Men were corrected and even called on the carpet; women who did something wrong were ignored because supervisors did not want to confront female executives. (Glenn Collins, "Unforeseen Business Barriers for Women," *New York Times*, May 31, 1982, p. A14.)

Hennig, Margaret, and Jardim, Anne. *The Managerial Woman.* New York: Anchor, 1981.

In part 1, these authors outline some of the "patterns of differences" between women's behavior as managers and men's and trace these patterns to differences in socialization, with special emphasis on women's lack of experience in team sports. Part 2 is a study of twenty-five successful women, most of whom put their "femininity on hold" during their early careers. Most identify with their fathers; most were first born, only children, or the eldest of sisters; all are now frozen in middle management. In part 3, the authors observe that none of us can change our birth order, redo our families, rework early relationships. What women can do to increase their own and one another's career success is spelled out in terms of first thinking hard and then taking hard actions, like going back to school to earn an M.B.A.

Horner, Matina. "Fail: Bright Women." *Psychology Today* 3, no. 6 (November 1969): 36–38; 62.

This is the pioneering study that showed some of the brightest young women could not envision themselves as successful. Many subsequent studies have found that men sometimes suffer from "fear of success" and certainly that not all women do. But Horner defined it first and she was clearly on to something.

Kleiman, Carol. *Women's Networks: The Complete Guide to Getting a Better Job, Advancing Your Career, and Feeling Great as a Woman through Networking.* New York: Ballantine, 1980.

This fine book (like Mary-Scott Welch's *Networking*) gives evidence that the best help women can get is from other women. It begins with the story of a network (club) of Chicago women at the top of their fields (Christie Hefner of *Playboy;* Evangeline Gouletas of American Invesco; Addie Wyatt of United Food and Commercial Workers, AFL-CIO; Mayor Jane Byrne; and others equally prominent and diverse) and how they got together. But it soon moves to ways in which women are helping one another not only professionally but personally. There are networks for women rearing children alone, for those coping with terminal diseases, for those trying to deal with chronic depression. Kleiman says the networks differ but they have one philosophy in common: there is always a way out of the tunnel, which women help one another find. In a lonely world, women are saving one another's lives.

Larwood, Laurie, and Lockheed, Marlaine. "Women as Managers: Toward Second Generation Research." *Sex Roles* 5, no. 5 (1979): 659–66.

These authors urge academics to turn to action-oriented research, calling for studies on productivity of women in nontraditional roles; analysis of techniques that women can use to get a management post; how they can obtain a pay increase, promotion, or needed training; how effective sex-segregated management training really is; which types of industrial organizations are providing the most supportive environments for women; and how affirmative action programs can be improved.

Larwood, Laurie, and Wood, Marion M. *Women in Management.* Lexington, Mass.: Lexington Books, 1977.

These authors review the body of literature that suggests women are encountering deep prejudice in their effort to climb the management ladder. In chapter 7 they offer alternative strategies as well as general tactics to help the reader achieve her goals. They do offer the "legal alternative," an option many do not choose to mention; they also offer fascinating details about the development of the case at Chase Manhattan Bank: how the women got together, how they fought the case; how they won.

Leavitt, Judith A. *Women in Management, 1970–1979: A Bibliography.* Chicago: CPL Bibliographies, 1980.

Good organization of material makes this a useful summary of available research. Leavitt's subtopics show the range of issues researchers have considered: progress of women in management; salaries, mentors and stereotypes; discrimination and minorities; education; profiles of women managers; career and family; women as directors of corporations; women "bosses"; recruiting women into management; obstacles women face; comparisons of men and women as managers; advice to women managers; women and the psychology of management; women managers in specific fields and various countries; general books on the topic; and bibliographies, of which hers is one of the best.

Loring, Rosalind, and Wells, Theodora. *Breakthrough: Women into Management.* New York: Van Nostrand, 1972.

This book is aimed at male managers, to spell out for them the legal requirements for providing equality of women workers and for modifying the organizational climate to ensure that women would be recruited, selected, trained, and promoted. Chapter 6 addresses the delicate relationship between new women managers and wives of men managers. These authors were well ahead of their time.

Martin, Judith. *Miss Manners' Guide to Excruciatingly Correct Behavior.* New York: Atheneum, 1982.

This 750-page book teaches the reader how to answer rudeness with politeness at every stage of the life cycle. Most pertinent for women managers are the sections on applying for jobs, raises, and fees; conducting business correspondence; and being a lady at work in an often chauvinist world. The guide (like Martin's nationally syndicated column) is framed in questions from gentle readers outlining their problems and Miss Manners' solutions to them, which are unfailingly sensible and delicious in their precision and wit. Manners never gives herself a title (her given name is Miss); she does not fail to write thank-you notes on appropriate paper; she does not flinch from giving advice on the most sensitive problems, from what to call out after an effective opera by gender and number ("Bravo" "Brava" or "Bravii") to how to behave when one is the boss's wife to his subordinates ("It is not pleasant for people to have close social relationships where there cannot be equality . . . [it is best to not push] friendliness beyond office-related social activities") to the tone one should take in a mimeographed Christmas letter ("Refrain from bragging . . . confine your news to more or less public matters—

'We've moved to Colorado' . . . 'Annabelle has joined the Army' . . . and state them neutrally . . .) to the way one should behave in a job interview ("Crispness replaces flirtatiousness" and here stating one's capabilities shows one to be an able worker, not a bragging bore.)

Miller, Casey, and Swift, Kate. *The Handbook of Nonsexist Writing for Writers, Editors, and Speakers.* New York: Barnes and Noble, 1981.

With crisp and strong examples, this 129-page guide directs writers and speakers away from unconscious semantic bias and toward clarity and fairness in language. It should be part of the kit of tools of any manager, woman or man. From the platform, in the memo, in the monthly report, we all sometimes still use phrases that reflect "old think": "farmers and their wives," "lady attorney," "male nurse." A useful index directs us to appropriate and inappropriate use of "black," "gal," "man," "female." The authors are respectful of people of all races and both sexes.

National Business Woman. Washington, D.C.: National Federation of Business and Professional Women's Clubs.

This bimonthly journal carries information of interest to women managers whether they are or are not members of BPW. The editors take pride in the fact that "Every BPW club is a management training program, and every BPW member has the opportunity to participate in some part of the training." The federation also publishes annotated bibliographies, reports of the research it sponsors, and other publications.

Nieva, Veronica F., and Gutek, Barbara A. *Women and Work: A Psychological Perspective.* New York: Praeger, 1981.

This is probably the most concise summary of what is known about women workers in general and women managers in particular. These two scholars evaluate research trends thoughtfully, concluding with the observation that the model one accepts to explain women's status dictates one's prescriptions for change. They categorize the models as (1) individual, (2) structural, (3) sex role, and (4) intergroup. The prescriptions these models suggest are, for the first, training for women; for the second, changes in organizational policy and practice; for the third, social change in sex role expectations; and for the fourth, networking and political action. None of these approaches could work alone. "Virtually every institution in society must change," they conclude, "to achieve equity at work."

O'Barr, William M., and Atkins, Bowman K. "'Women's Language' or 'Powerless Language'?" In *Women and Language in Literature and Society,* edited by Sally McConnell-Ginet, Ruth Borker, and Nelly Furman, pp. 93–110. New York: Praeger, 1980.

These anthropologists recorded 150 hours of trials in a North Carolina superior criminal court looking for ten features believed to be characteristic of women's speech: hedges, superpolite forms, tag questions, speaking in italics, empty adjectives, hypercorrect grammar and pronunciation, lack of a sense of humor, direct quotations, special lexicon, and question intonation in declarative contexts. They found that not all women exhibit these features in their speech and that some men do, concluding that such usages were related to social position rather than to sex. They present evidence that persons of either sex who exhibit these characteristics "tend to be judged as less convincing, less truthful, less competent, less intelligent, and less trustworthy" than those who don't.

O'Reilly, Jane. *The Girl I Left Behind.* New York: Bantam, 1982.

Journalist O'Reilly contributed a piece on housework to the first issue of *Ms.*; lectured on women's issues in the mid-seventies; interviewed traditionalist Phyllis Schlafly at the 1977 National Women's Conference in Houston; sat in on the Senate hearings on a constitutional amendment to ban abortion; traced the fights in the state legislatures that resulted in the defeat of the Equal Rights Amendment; and analyzed the effect of President Ronald Reagan's policies on women. This book is a collection of reflections, almost all of them astute and wry and sound, on the decade of the 1970s. She notes that unless we keep our wits about us, American society will move toward the "Greek model" with women going out to work and caring for home and children while the men keep the power and sit about in cafes discussing politics all day. Sometimes she wishes wistfully for a Rich Husband, considering that her friends who have one "toil not, neither do they spin, instead they spend." But mostly, she celebrates women's progress. She was especially interested in the settlement of the class action sex discrimination suit at the *New York Times.* The *Times* gave the grievants $233,500, which it insisted on calling an "annuity program" to "compensate some women for societal discrimination. . . ." The grievants saw those payments, which were cashable immediately, as back pay in recompense for sex discrimination they had put up with at the *Times.*

Pepper, William F., and Kennedy, Florynce R. *Sex Discrimination in Employment.* Charlottesville, Va.: Michie Bobbs-Merrill, 1982.

Newly out at this writing, this law book is lauded by Honorable Leonard N. Cohen, acting supreme court justice of the state of New York, as a "thorough, concise and pioneering practical guide." There is no talk of "managing liability" in this book. It is aimed at lawyers who want to make corporations liable and responsible for their treatment of women. Includes sample litigation forms for filing a class action suit under Title VII and an interesting epilogue warning the "world's largest minority" not to expect too much too soon from the judiciary—discrimination on the basis of sex is deep-seated and irrational. Kennedy says, "... the Establishment should be worried about the antiestablishmentarians—the women, the Blacks, the youth, the aged, all the people who have no full part in the system, those I call the 'niggers' of this country. They are planning campaigns in each legislative district. They are moving out of the streets and into the executive suites." This quote, together with some of Kennedy's other items of verbal karate ("If men could get pregnant, abortion would be a sacrament"), is an example of the treasures to be found in a second useful reference book: Elaine Partnow's *The Quotable Woman: An Encyclopedia of Useful Quotations Indexed by Subject and Author, 1800–On* (Garden City, N.Y.: Anchor Books, 1978).

Piercy, Day. "Working Mothers/Parents: Recommended Corporate Policies." Chicago: Women Employed Institute, 1981.

This 8-page publication offers a series of suggested policies on sick leave, personal leave, adoption leave, phone calls at work, part-time work, and job-sharing, which, if implemented, might well ease the career-home conflicts faced by women workers at all levels. The Women Employed Institute (5 South Wabash, Suite 415, Chicago, IL 60603) offers a series of publications, including "Discrimination at Harris Trust & Savings Bank: An Updated Case Study," "Survival Manual for Insurance Women," "Helpful Hints for the New Working Mother," and "Working Woman's Cookbook," the last two written by working mothers.

Rowe, Mary P. "Dealing with Sexual Harassment." *Harvard Business Review* 59, no. 3 (May–June 1981): 42–44; 46.

Concrete suggestions for handling gross problems.

Shaeffer, Ruth Gilbert, and Lynton, Edith F. *Corporate Experiences in Improving Women's Job Opportunities.* A Research Report from the Conference Board. New York: Conference Board, 1979.

How did the corporations surveyed increase the representation of women managers? Six tactics were reported: commitment from top management; accountability of line managers for EEO results; increased influence on staffing by corporate personnel departments and EEO staff; ability to recruit an ample supply of qualified women, both externally and internally; training line managers in interviewing, selecting, and training women candidates; and ensuring that women acquired the knowledge and skills required for promotion.

Shreve, Anita. "Careers and the Lure of Motherhood." *New York Times Magazine,* November 21, 1982, pp. 38–56.

An interesting roundup of ways women executives cope with child care. Ten years ago, the article might well have raised the question a different way: When can mothers succumb to the lure of working and go back? One mother quoted remarked that nowadays the question is not *either* a career *or* a family but how.

Thompson, Ann McKay, and Wood, Marcia Donnan. *Management Strategies for Women: Now That I'm Boss, How Do I Run This Place?* New York: Touchstone, Simon and Schuster, 1982.

A potpourri of games, quizzes, lists of maxims, commandments, and, as the authors say in the introduction, humor. The latter is sadly lacking in much standard advice to would-be managers. Especially rcommended: chapter 12, "Zap Quiz"; chapter 15, "Avoiding Tooth-Fairy Economics"; and chapter 17, which is a guide to conducting meetings, often a special challenge for women newly in supervisory positions.

Trahey, Jane. *Jane Trahey on Women and Power.* New York: Avon, 1977.

What kind of image do corporate men have of women? Advertising executive Trahey checked it out by reviewing all Fortune 500 annual reports, looking for pictures of women and counting women listed as board members. The results of that study are reported in this lively book, together with her interviews of successful women. The interviewees identified with their mothers; they spoke to her quite candidly about their work which they clearly relish. If she is smart-alecky in tone and, from time to time, a tad irresponsible in reporting, this is still a good book. She has sensible advice on getting credit for your good ideas, for dealing with "sex and booze power ploys," and the like.

Welch, Mary-Scott. *Networking: The Great New Way for Women to Get Ahead.* New York: Warner, 1981.

One of two excellent books (see also Carol Kleiman, *Women's Networks*) which tell concretely how women are really helping other women. This one focuses on how women are giving and getting information on work problems: what to do, for instance, when you get a bad performance evaluation in a big corporation; how to comport yourself when you are being ground up in political struggles in the office; how to get information through a network on how much money people at your level in other departments and other companies are earning. The book gives tips on avoiding pitfalls: how to avoid exploiting one another; when a women's network may evolve into something else; how to avert the tyranny of too much Mickey-Mouse structure and the anarchy of structurelessness. Some networks are secret; others, up front; some are political, others can't be. Women's organizations and what they are up to inside Equitable Life, Polaroid, NBC, and other companies are described.

West, Candace. "Why Can't a Woman Be More Like a Man? An Interactional Note on Organizational Game-Playing for Managerial Women." *Work and Occupations* 9, no. 1 (February 1982): 5–29.

A linguist's analysis of men's and women's problems in conversation. For example, men interrupt women much more than vice versa, men tend not to listen to women's ideas, and so on. The author feels that assertiveness training for women is not the answer to this problem: "'Assertiveness' is implicated in interactions *between* people: to focus 'sensitization' efforts only on women is not only to blame the victim but also of dubious pragmatic value."

Wheeler-Bennett, Joan. *Women at the Top: Achievement and Family Life.* London: Peter Owen, 1977.

This book consists of reports of interviews with fifteen successful women. The descriptions of the way the women look are embarrassing but the reports of the husbands' responses to questions posed to them are enlightening. Each woman was asked if her sex was an advantage in her line of work in Britain. The social worker, civil servant, novelist, publisher, architect, journalist, headmistress, barrister, and those in public relations, market research, advertising, and medicine reported various advantages. The biochemist had a one-word answer to the question: no.

Whelan, Elizabeth M. "Confessions of a 'Superwoman'." *Across the Board* 17, no. 12 (December 1980): 17–25.

The author was asked when she graduated from high school what she aspired to have in twenty years. Her goals were four: a good education, a husband, a child, and a beautiful suburban home. By 1980, she had all those things plus a demanding career as a Harvard University research associate and author of eleven books, among them, *A Baby? . . . Maybe: A Guide To Making the Most Fateful Decision of Your Life* (New York: Bobbs-Merrill, 1976). But the bubble burst. She couldn't do everything at once. Could her attorney husband cut back to half time? Nonsense. "Most professional men today do not have the sort of job freedom to allow more participation in parenthood." Her career was more flexible than his; she cut back. "The day I faced the necessity for modifying and realigning those life goals made long ago was a most difficult one for me because, in essence, I had discovered my limits."

Whisner, Mary. "Gender-Specific Clothing Regulation: A Study in Patriarchy." *Harvard Women's Law Journal* 5 (Spring 1982): 73–119.

From Eve's fig leaf through the bras that were never burned at the 1968 Miss America pageant and from Amelia Bloomer's decision to wear pantaloons under her ankle-length skirt to "dress for success," feminists who concern themselves with clothing have been either dismissed as frivolous or attacked as a menace to the family and the natural order of things. Whisner's thoughtful review is exceedingly interesting. Airline attendants, nuns, police officers, cocktail servers, and nurses have long known what corporate women are learning: you are not what you wear but you are often seen to be.

Wolf, Wendy C., and Fligstein, Neil D. "Sex and Authority in the Workplace: The Causes of Sexual Inequality." *American Sociological Review* 44 (April 1979): 235–52.

These researchers surveyed 5,613 employed men and women in 1975. Defining authority as the ability to hire or fire others, to influence or set their pay rates, and to supervise the work of others, they found that men were much more likely to have authority than women were. They hypothesized that this gap might be due to three factors: women's qualifications, the behaviors and policies of employers, or the attitudes and behaviors of women. Their analysis suggests that some of the gap in authority can be explained by the first factor and some by the third but that the second is most important.

Working Woman Success Book by the editors of *Working Woman* Magazine. New York: Ace, Grosset & Dunlap, 1981.

Articles which have appeared in her magazine are introduced by editor Kate Rand Lloyd. In her introduction, Lloyd remarked that her own career had taught her that certain notions have hidden meanings. "Be loyal to the company" means "Don't quit to get a better job," and "Be sweet and conscientious and your virtue will be rewarded" really means that a pat on the head costs nothing. Of special interest are Shirley Sloan Fader's "The Answers to Tough Interview Questions" and Victoria Pellegrino's "Office Politics: Running a Clean Campaign." Energy and excitement sparkle out of many of these articles. Getting a really good job won't resolve all problems; indeed, it may even create some. But it helps. Success, they say, is not to be feared.

Index

A Baby? . . . Maybe, 94
Academy of Management,
    Interest Group on Women, vi
Acceptance, by men of women
    managers, 47
Action-oriented research, need
    for, 87
Adams, Jane, 80
Administrative Science Quarterly,
    35
Adoption leave, 91
Aetna Life & Casualty
    Foundation, v
Affirmative action, 38, 83, 87;
    officers, 41
*Affirmative Action and the
    Woman Worker: Guidelines
    for Personnel Management,* 83
Aggression, fear of, 37
American Association of
    University Women, Ithaca
    Branch, vi
American Home Economics
    Association, vi
American Telephone and
    Telegraph Corporation
    (AT&T), 78
Antiestablishmentarians, women
    managers as among the, 91
"Application of Title VII to Jobs
    in High Places," 80
Assertiveness training, 76, 93
Atkins, Bowman K., 90
Authority gap, between women
    and men managers, 94

Balancing career and family
    responsibilities, 10
Bank of America, 78
Bartlett, Linda, viii, 40–44
Bartholet, Elizabeth, 80
Basil, Douglas C., 81

Becket, Thomas à, 27
Benefits, 4, 52, 59, 64, 82
Bingham, Roger, 75
Bird, Caroline, 78, 81
Black, being, 39, 41
Blanchard, Kenneth, 78
Bonding, instinct for, 74
Borker, Ruth, 90
*Boss Lady: An Executive Woman
    Talks about Making It,* 83
Boss, relationship of subordinate
    to, 18
Brain functioning, male/female
    difference in, 75
*Breakthrough: Women into
    Management,* 88
*Bringing Women into
    Management,* 78, 84
Britain, women managers in, 93
Brown, Linda Keller, 74, 81
Business and Professional
    Women's Clubs: Ithaca, vi;
    National Federation of, 89
Business and Professional
    Women's Foundation, 81
Business Games Quotient, 15–16
Byrnes, Eleanor, viii, 49–53,
    69, 70
Byrne, Jane, 87

"Cafeteria style" benefits, 52, 59
Career planning, 2, 76
Chase Manhattan Bank, 78, 87
Child care, 54–56, 82, 92; as
    benefit, 4; corporate
    sponsored, 52, 59, 62; costs of,
    55; full-time housekeeper to
    provide, 66–67; leave, 50
Children, as topic of
    conversation, 35–36
Citrino, Mary Anne, 1
Cinderella Complex, 75

Class action suits, 44, 78, 91
Clothes, favored by women
    managers, 35, 69, 76
Coffey, Margaret, viii, 61–64, 71
Cohen, Leonard N., 91
Comparable pay for work of
    comparable value, 5, 10
"Confessions of a 'Superwoman',"
    94
Continental Illinois National
    Bank and Trust Company, 49
Cook, Alice H., 69
Cornell Society of Women
    Engineers, vi
Cornell Women in
    Communications, vi
Cornell Women's Caucus, vi
Cornell Women's Club of
    Tompkins County, vi
Cornell Women's Studies
    Program, vi
Corporate Experiences in
    Improving Women's Job
    Opportunities, 92
"Corporate feminism," 84
Corporate values, 52–53
Corporations and Two-Career
    Families, 82
Criticism of women bosses, 35, 36

Data General, 22
"Dealing with Sexual
    Harassment," 91
Demographic changes, 4, 5
Digital Equipment, 22, 29
Discretion, as characteristic of
    powerful job, 29
Displacement of male workers by
    females, alleged, 9
Dowling, Colette, 74–75
"Dressed for Success: The New
    Corporate Feminism," 84
Drucker, Peter, 3
Dual career couples, 49–53

Economy, effect of changes on
    women, 6–7, 14; effecting
    changes in, 10
Education: advanced degrees, 2;
    business schools, 5; changes in
    undergraduate, 5

Effective Woman Manager, The,
    76
Epstein, Cynthia Fuchs, 84
Equal employment opportunity,
    92; evaluating companies, 82;
    officers, 41
Equal Employment Opportunity
    Commission (EEOC), 40
Equal Rights Amendment (ERA),
    13, 19, 20, 34, 90; effect on
    homemakers, 9–10
Equitable Life, 93
Everything a Woman Needs to
    Know to Get Paid What She's
    Worth . . . in the 1980's, 81

Fader, Shirley Sloan, 82, 95
"Fail: Bright Women," 86
Families at Work: Strengths and
    Strains, 82
Farley, Jennie, v–ix, 69–95
Father, identification of women
    managers with, 86
Fear of success, 75, 83, 86
Feminization of corporations, 20
Field, Anne, 74
Flexplace, 51, 59
Flextime, 10, 51, 59
Fligstein, Neil D., 94
Forisha, Barbara L., 83
Fortune 500 companies' annual
    reports, 92
Fortune 1300 corporations,
    survey of, 82
Foxworth, Jo, 78, 83
Furman, Nelly, 90

Games Mother Never Taught You,
    12, 14, 78
Gender Advertisements, 84
Gender gap in voting patterns, 20
"Gender-Specific Clothing
    Regulation," 94
Ginzberg, Eli, 49–50
Girl I Left Behind, The, 78, 90
Gittelson, Natalie, 77
Godfrey, Marjorie, 78, 81
Goffman, Erving, 84
Goldman, Barbara H., 83
Goodmeasure, Inc., 21, 34
Gordon, Francine E., 78, 84

Gordon, Suzanne, 84
Gornick, Vivian, 84
Gouletas, Evangeline, 87
Greenwald, Carol S., 74, 85
Gutek, Barbara A., 89
Gutreimer, Janne, 75n

Hall, Douglas T., 85
Hall, Francine S., 85
Handbook of Nonsexist Writing for Writers, Editors, and Speakers, The, 89
Harragan, Betty Lehan, vii, 12–19, 47, 78
Harris Trust & Savings Bank, 91
Harvard University, 2, 94
Harlan, Anne, 86
Hefner, Christine, 87
Hennig, Margaret, 78, 86
Hewlett-Packard, 22
Home, working at, 71. *See also* Flexplace
Horner, Matina, 75, 86
Housework, 90
Human Resource Division of New York City, 40
Human resource management. *See* Personnel
Human Rights Commission of New York State, 40
Husband's participation in child care and home tasks, 70

IBM Corporation, v
ILR Women's Caucus, vi
Insurance women, 91
Internal placement network, 51
Interviews, 15, 41, 95
Ithaca (NY) *Journal*, 37

Jacklin, Carol Nagy, 84
Jane Trahey on Women and Power, 78, 92
Jardim, Anne, 78, 86
Job sharing, 91
Johnson, Pam McAllister, viii, 37–39
Johnson, Spencer, 78

Kanter, Rosabeth Moss, viii, 21–33, 78

Kennedy, Florynce R., 91
Kidder, Tracy, 23–24
Kiryluk, Carol, viii, 45–48
Kleiman, Carol, 87, 93
Kleiman, Dina, 2n
Kosinar, Patricia, 83
Kreps, Juanita M., vi, 1–11, 78

Labor market, changing, 4
Ladies' room, absence of, 42
Language, 17–18, 89, 90
Larwood, Laurie, 78, 87
Law schools, increase in women enrolled, 5
Leaves, 50, 91
Leavitt, Judith, 74, 88
Legal rights of women, 82
Line jobs, 16
Litigation, as strategy of last resort, 41
Lloyd, Kate Rand, 95
Lockheed, Marlaine, 87
Loneliness, as problem of single women managers, 46
Loring, Rosalind, 88
Lynton, Edith F., 92

Maccoby, Eleanor Emmons, 84
McConnell-Ginet, Sally, 90
Management Strategies for Women, 77, 92
Management training for women, 14, 81
Managerial Mind, The, 76
Managerial Woman, The, 78, 86
Mandelbaum, Helen, 78, 81
Martin, Judith, 88
Maternity leave, 2, 50–51
Math avoidance, 75
M.B.A. degree, 50, 62, 81, 86
Media, image of women in, 3, 13, 84
Meeting, conducting a, 92
Men and Women of the Corporation, 21, 25, 78
Mentors, 31, 47, 80
Middle managers, 38
Military: as similar to business, 16; language in business, 17
Miller, Casey, 89
Minority women, 39, 41, 69

*Miss Manners' Guide to
Excruciatingly Correct
Behavior,* 88
Mobility: internal, 24; problems
of managers, 4, 52
Mobil Oil Corporation, v
Moore, Mary Ellen, 78
Moral Majority, ix, 9
Mortarboard, Cornell
University, vi
Motivation of woman managers,
as often questioned, 15
*Moving Up: Women in
Managerial Careers,* 86

Names, 83
National Business Woman, 89
National Organization for
Women (NOW), Tompkins
County, NY, vi
NBC, 93
Nepotism rules, 50, 82
Networking, 87, 93
New Executive Woman, The, 76
New right, effect on women's
opportunities, 9
New York State Governor's Office
of Employee Relations and the
Civil Service Association Joint
Labor/Management
Committee on the Work
Environment and Productivity
(CWEP), v
New York State School of
Industrial and Labor Relations,
vi
New York Times, 1, 78, 90
Nieva, Veronica F., 89
Northwestern Medical School, 51

O'Barr, William M., 90
Oesterle, Patricia M., viii, 54–56, 70
Office politics, 95
Office romance, 83
One-Minute Manager, The, 78
O'Reilly, Jane, 78, 90
Osterman, Gail Bryant, viii,
57–60
*Outsiders on the Inside: Women
and Organizations,* 83

Parenting, attitude toward, 60
Participative management, 83
Partnow, Elaine, 91
Part-time work, 2, 10, 51–52,
59–60, 63–64, 91
Paternity leave, 70
Patronage system, 31
Pay gap, between women's salary
and men's, 10, 15, 73–74
Pellegrino, Victoria, 95
Pepper, William F., 91
*Personal and Professional Success
for Women,* 76
Personnel: importance in
declining economy, 47–48;
upward mobility in, 46
Piercy, Day, 91
Polaroid, 93
Power, 7, 21–33, 76
Powerlessness, 26, 27–28, 90
Powerless boss, coping with, 35
Pregnancy, 51, 52, 83
Princeton University, 1, 2
Professionalism, 35
Professional Skills Roster, vi
Provost's Advisory Committee on
the Status of Women at
Cornell University, vi

Queen Bee syndrome, 74
Quill & Dagger, Cornell
University, vi
Quotable Woman, The, 91

Racism, avoiding in language, 89
Radcliffe College, 2
Raise, asking for, 16, 83–84, 88.
See also Salary
Reagan, Ronald, 90
Records, importance of keeping,
43
Recruitment, 83
Rehmus, Charles, vi
Relevance, as characteristic of
powerful job, 30
Relocation, problems of, 4–5,
46–47, 82
Reporting relationships, 22
Results-oriented management
skills, 69–70

Retirement benefits, 4
Reverse discrimination, 9
Risk: asking sponsor to take, 32; necessity of taking, 48, 76
Rivlin, Alice, 6
Routes to the Executive Suite, 76
Rowe, Mary P., 91
Rytina, Nancy F., 74n

Salary, importance of thinking about, 18
Sales work, as example of line job, 20
Schlafly, Phyllis, 90
Science, 75
Security, employment, 24
Selection methods, 80, 83
Settlement, internal, importance of, 41
"Sex and Authority in the Workplace," 94
Sex discrimination, 13; as disease, 14; examples of, 42; subtle forms of, 85
Sex Discrimination in Employment, 91
Sexual harassment, 10–11, 42–43, 78, 91, 92–93
Shaeffer, Ruth Gilbert, 92
Shreve, Anita, 92
Silcox, Diana, 78
Single woman manager, 45–48
Slogans, corporate, 38
Smith, Deborah K., viii, 65–68
"Socialization and Self Esteem: Women in Management," 83
Society for the Advancement of Management, Syracuse University Chapter, vi
Soul of a New Machine, The, 24
Sponsors, 31, 32
Sports: use of language in business, 17, 18; women in, 15, 83, 86. *See also* Team
Spouse employment network, 50
Staff jobs, 16
Staines, Graham, 74
Stereotypes, about women professionals, 3, 71
Stress, experienced by working mothers, 62, 80

Strober, Myra H., 78, 84
Subordinates, as source of power, 32
Successfully Ever After: A Young Woman's Guide to Career Happiness, 82
Superwoman, 56, 69, 94
Sweden, 60
Swift, Kate, 89
Symons, Donald, 75

"Tale of O," 34
Team: difficulty of getting on the, 32; meaning of, 17–18, 24
Tests, assessment, 82
"That's No Lady, That's My Boss," 37
Theory X, 78
Theory Y, 78
Thompson, Ann McKay, 77, 92
Tiger, Lionel, 74
Time management, importance of, 67
Title IX of the Education Amendments Act of 1972, 13
Title VII of the Civil Rights Act, 13, 80
Tooth-Fairy economics, 92
Top managerial ranks, as bereft of women, 52, 73
Trahey, Jane, 78, 92
Transfers, 4–5, 45–47
Travel: necessity for, 52; problems with, 59
Traver, Edna, 81
Two-Career Couple, The, 85
Two-Paycheck Marriage, The, 81

Unions, 81
United Food and Commercial Workers, 87
U.S. Cabinet, women in, vii
University Lecture Committee, Cornell, vi

Values, personal, 54
Van Gelder, Lindsy, 79n
Visibility, as characteristic of powerful job, 29

Weiss, Carol, 86
Welch, Mary-Scott, 87, 93
Wells, Theodora, 88
Weisstein, Naomi, 75
Weslock, Kathleen, v
West, Candace, 93
Western Electric, 78
Wheeler-Bennett, Joan, 93
Whelan, Elizabeth M., 94
Whisner, Mary, 94
"Why Can't a Woman Be More
 Like a Man?" 93
Wising Up: The Mistakes Women
 Make in Business and How to
 Avoid Them, 78, 83
Wives of managers and women
 managers, relationship
 between, 88
Wolf, Wendy C., 94
Womantime: Personal Time
 Management for Women Only,
 78
Women and Language in
 Literature and Society, 90
Women and the American
 Economy, 78
Women and Work: A
 Psychological Perspective, 89
"Women and Work" seminars, at
 bank, 51
"Women as Managers: Toward
 Second Generation Research,"
 87
Women at the Top: Achievement
 and Family Life, 93
Women Employed Institute, 91
Women in Management, 78, 81,
 85, 87

Women in Management,
 1970–1979: A Bibliography, 88
Women on Top: Success Patterns
 and Personal Growth, 80
Women's Association, Graduate
 School of Business and Public
 Administration, Cornell
 University, vi
Women's conferences, 12
"'Women's Language' or
 'Powerless Language'?" 90
Women's Law Coalition, Cornell
 University, vi
Women's Networks..., 87, 93
Wood, Marcia Donnan, 77, 92
Wood, Marion M., 78, 87
Working Mothers/Parents:
 Recommended Corporate
 Policies, 91
Working Woman Success Book,
 95
"Working Woman's Cookbook,"
 91
World War II, 5, 9
Wyatt, Addie, 87

Xerox Corporation, v, 65

Yankelovich, Daniel, 38
Yale University, courses for
 managers at, 36

"Zap Quiz," 92
Zeitz, Baila, 82
Zonta of Ithaca, vi